Praise for *The Path To Stillness*

With Adam Brady's real-life experience of transformation via meditation, combined with his rich education and teaching in the field, he is uniquely able to inform and compel a reader toward the profound timeless practice like few others. With a topic that can often be difficult to grasp, the clarity of his writing style, and the way information is presented, makes reading this book especially enjoyable, informative and truly inspiring.
    —*Amanda Ree, Chopra Certified Vedic Educator & Founder of Sama Dog: Wellbeing for Dogs + Their Humans*

On my quest for inner peace and a quiet mind, Adam Brady has been extremely beneficial and helpful as a guide for me. He's made meditation easy to accept and understand and he's been extremely encouraging and supportive along the way. I am grateful for his guidance and continued support.
    —*Jonathan Burke, Head Coach, Tactical Jiu-Jitsu Instructor at The VI Levels Orlando and Royce Gracie's 1st black belt*

Opening this guide is like sitting down with an old friend and having a spiritual retreat from the comfort of wherever you're reading. Adam has successfully transcribed his live training into a tool to be shared broadly. I have leveraged Adam's expertise throughout the years in a corporate wellness setting and have first-handedly seen the positive impact of his training on our employees and business as a whole.
    —*Sarah Popiel, Wellness Program Manager*

I have been blessed to know Adam Brady for nearly the last decade of my martial and meditation career and practice. His knowledge and experience in one arena have led him to new discoveries in the other, and vice versa.

In *The Path to Stillness*, Adam delivers a text that provides insights that both novice and experienced meditators can turn to. His applications of the philosophy of Jeet Kune Do and its strategic concept of attacking before, during, or after an opponent's movement to dealing with thought gives martial artists looking to deepen their practice an avenue that integrates body and mind. I highly recommend this book to anyone interested in developing a meditative practice, and specifically for martial artists.

Now, if you'll excuse me, I must go practice my mantra; "Om Cherry Cheese Danish"

—JB MuSsang Jaeger, *Maryland Jeet Kune Do*

The Path to Stillness is an amazingly comprehensive instruction manual for those new to meditation. It includes a thorough presentation of what meditation is and is not, how meditation is different than mindfulness, the mind-body connection, and meditation's physiological effects on the body. Once that foundation is complete, Adam skillfully, simply, and clearly guides the reader through the meditation practice, including suggestions for variations and additions that can deepen the reader's experience. And while the book is so clear, simple, and thorough, Adam's voice is the perfect, gentle guide—encouraging, eloquent, humorous, and wise. You will feel calm just reading this book. He is gentle and assuring, strong and pragmatic, and experienced and confident. You can feel his support of YOUR meditation journey, and you will feel empowered to practice and succeed!

—Melissa Feldman, *Holistic Health Practitioner, Yoga, Meditation, Breathing, and Zen Shiatsu Instructor*

In *The Path to Stillness*, those who are new to meditation are left with no choice but to join Adam in his pursuit to physical, emotional and spiritual stillness. With the deftness honoring the education background of his parents, the reader is able to clearly understand the why and how of incorporating a meditation practice into their own lives. This book has been well thought out, is easy to read, AND a must read for those who are looking to experience a more colorful and fulfilling life.
    —Laura Giancarlo, Science and Health Educator, Martial
        Artist, student of mediation and acupressure therapy
        and Resilience Coach/Mentor in training

Stillness is a superpower! In his book, *The Path to Stillness*, Adam Brady clearly lays out the foundations of the process of meditation. Everyone has tried meditation, and most have failed. The reason for failure comes down to not having proper guidelines and expectations of the practice. Adam clearly lays out the why's and how's of mediation so that the practitioner can get a clear understanding of the process and benefits gained from a daily practice.

    Adam is a master of his craft, never missing a day of meditation in over 22 years. Through his experiences with some of the greats like Deepak Chopra and his study of Martial Arts he has a unique perspective and first-hand knowledge of implementing a successful mediation practice. Finally, you don't have to abandon everything and run away to the top of a mountain to meet a master in a cave who will show you the way. I highly recommend this book; it has functional gems that will transform not only your performance but your life!
    —*Sifu Harinder Singh*
        Kung Fu Master, Author, & High-Performance Coach

I have known Adam for many years and he always exuded calm, and dare I use the word – Zen. Adam has long forged a path of knowing himself in a deeper manner than simply accepting "I am who I am ". While important to know thyself, it is important to want to dig deeper and be more to thyself and the world. To me this is who Adam is – always digging and asking more from himself.

I found Adam's book to be easy to read. I like the layout of his book from the definition of mediation to the benefits and structure of mediation. Adam has created a book that is easy to share with clients because it is easy for the busy individual to review, implement, and if so inclined, further understand the art of meditation and the range of benefits from this practice.

I particularly like how he makes meditation approachable. It is a valuable tool that anyone can access, implement any time, day or night, and it never expires. The mystery has been removed but the value of mediation remains.

Mediation is something I look forward to for it is the one or two times in my day the world stops spinning for a moment and I can just be. Adam's book is clear about the benefits and ease of mediation. I no longer feel guilty about falling asleep if I mediate, I can simply pick up where I left of and just be me.

—*Kate Miller, Associate Certified Coach, Executive Coach*

The Path to Stillness is simply the best darn book that I've read on the subject of meditation, period! In it Adam defines what meditation is, how to do it, and most importantly why a person should want to meditate. The book addresses the subject thoroughly and concisely in language that is straightforward and easy to read. It is packed with modern research on the subject and flavored with the ancient philosophy that we associate with contemplative practices. The book is light-hearted and humorous in one moment then deeply profound in the next. A true joy to read! I wish I had it when I started my meditation practice forty years ago.

—*John Giancarlo, Jin Shin Jyutsu Acupressure Therapist, LMT*
   Senior Master Level Martial Arts instructor, Educator, and
   forty-year practitioner of Japanese and Tibetan meditation

THE PATH TO STILLNESS

Also by Adam Brady

Warrior of Light

THE PATH TO STILLNESS

A Meditator's Guide

Adam Brady

Revised Reality Press
Winter Garden, Florida

The Path to Stillness: A Meditator's Guide
© 2019, Adam Brady. All rights reserved.

Published by Revised Reality Press, Winter Garden, Florida

ISBN 978-1-7346052-0-4 (paperback)
ISBN 978-1-7346052-1-1 (eBook)
Library of Congress Control Number: 2020904193

RevisedReality.com

Without limiting the rights under copyright reserved above, no part of this publication may be reproduced, stored in or introduced into a retrieval system, or transmitted in any form or by any means (electronic, mechanical, photocopying, recording or otherwise), without the prior written permission of both the copyright owner and the above publisher of this book, except by a reviewer who wishes to quote brief passages in connection with a review written for insertion in a magazine, newspaper, broadcast, website, blog or other outlet.

This book is intended to provide accurate information with regards to its subject matter. However, in times of rapid change, ensuring all information provided is entirely accurate and up-to-date at all times is not always possible. Therefore, the author and publisher accept no responsibility for inaccuracies or omissions and specifically disclaim any liability, loss or risk, personal, professional or otherwise, which may be incurred as a consequence, directly or indirectly, of the use and/ or application of any of the contents of this book.

Publishing consultant: David Wogahn, AuthorImprints.com

DEDICATION

For my parents, who encouraged my curiosity, creativity, and the desire to be a good and decent human being, even as I left the tribe to chase after the truth in Meditation, Yoga, Martial Arts, and Mind-Body Wellness.

For my brother Matt, whose writing and teaching have inspired me to think critically, write honestly, teach passionately, and still be a big goof at heart.

For my wife Dana, who was willing to give up our time together so I could study, train, teach, and eventually write this thing. You are my world, without whom all my running around would mean nothing. There's no one I'd rather stand on a fairytale castle stage with.

For my past teachers and students – you have shaped my thoughts and actions that have led me to this present moment. For the teachers and students I have yet to meet, you keep me learning and improving on a journey of personal growth and evolution.

Thank you all.

INSIDE

Foreword iii
Introduction 1

PART 1: WHAT IS MEDITATION, AND HOW DO I DO IT? 13
What is Meditation? 15
What You Can Expect 35
The Four Pillars of Meditation 51

PART 2: WHAT ARE THE BENEFITS? 59
The Physical Benefits of Meditation 61
The Mental and Emotional Benefits of Meditation 81
The Spiritual Benefits of Meditation 105
Performance Benefits 145

PART 3: BUILDING A PRACTICE 163
Creating a Successful Meditation Practice 165
Taking Your Practice Deeper 189
Meditation to Shape New Beliefs 225
An End to Suffering 235

Conclusion 243
Suggested Reading 245
Notes 247
Meditation Log 249
Acknowledgements 251
About the Author 253
Also By Adam Brady 254

FOREWORD

The world around us is rippling with activity. We are in constant dynamic exchange with nature. Storms roll through the oceans of the planet gifting us wind and rain which becomes our breath . . . feeding the forests and valleys . . . fueling the birds and animals . . . in turn nourishing the plants . . . creating a haven for insects . . . flitting from leaf to flower . . . feeding sweet mother earth, which then birth the next seeds of life.

In the concrete jungles of our cities, electricity races through buildings, homes & roads lighting the path each day for 8 billion humans to commune, work, play & travel like moths to a flame. We fill the precious spaces between each active moment with idle conversation, movement born of anxiety & nervousness, and hypnotic gazes into our beloved devices. We spend so much of our lives reinforcing conditioned behaviors & mindless pre-occupations that we are rarely ever aware that we are ignoring the richness of our lives.

Yet, this magnificence is there for the taking . . . resting deep inside you . . . patiently waiting to be awakened amidst the swirl & noise of the world around us—fully available and offered freely to you . . . if you can just figure out where to look. And, if we are fortunate—at some defining moment in our life—we feel a spark, we sense a calling, we see a sign, we hear a voice . . . and the journey of discovery & deeper meaning begins. That is why you are here . . . . That moment is now.

The most ancient wisdom traditions teach us that there is a space between all the thoughts, sensations, and experiences that flow into us and the subsequent responses we flow back into the world using our words and actions. Modern science has recently confirmed this law of human nature. Mostly, we ignore that space, and we react with some conditioned behavior, phrase, or expression. Sometimes, our hormones and chemicals drive our conduct in a mindless or thoughtless way. And though we don't control what life delivers to us in each moment . . . in that space between what comes in and what goes out, rests the present moment where we actually get to choose our response. And what we do with that moment and all the other ones like it throughout the course of the day . . . ultimately becomes the fabric of our life.

Over the past decade, clinical research has cited meditation as a powerful tool to help us find that space . . . to stay in it a bit longer . . . and to make more mindful and thoughtful choices. Once we learn how to cultivate this innate ability, it begins to weave itself into every aspect of our being so we can live each moment with greater clarity . . . transcend our conditioned responses . . . and show up as our best version.

You are here right now reading these words because you are at one of these defining moments in your life . . . you know that both powerful transformation & deeper fulfillment await you on the path to your higher Self. And so right now might be the perfect time to heed the call, trust your inner voice, and take that long-awaited step toward your best version.

I believe that authentic personal transformation comes from a divine convergence of Message, Messenger, and Timing. When that perfect fusion is realized, a life-changing moment unfolds. If one of those core elements is missing, it's just another moment. But, if the message resonates with you . . . and it flows from the lips of a trusted source AND you are in a space where you are ready to receive the message from that source . . . BOOM! . . . transformation is inescapable.

We've already established that you are ready, because you are here right now. And we know the message is resonating with you because you have taken your first step on the journey to stillness. And so, it all comes down to the messenger—Adam Brady.

FOREWORD

Adam has been exactly where you are in this moment. Curious . . . innocent . . . unsure . . . and showing up with a beginner's mind. He knew that if he could access that space between his thoughts, between his words, between his actions . . . then he could use that stillness between activity to find balance, manage his stress, be the calm amidst the chaos of daily life, and make better personal choices, more purposeful career choices, and more rewarding life choices.

Like many of us, he took his first step by dipping his toe into the vast ocean of timeless wisdom teachings and then began to see the world with new eyes. He started a daily practice and committed himself more deeply to the study of meditation. But his insatiable desire to live the teachings at a deeper level inspired him to enroll in a program to become a certified teacher. At the time, I was the dean of Chopra Center University and there were hundreds of students each year going through our program. But very quickly, Adam distinguished himself from the pack. His thirst to learn the subtleties and nuances of meditation was unquenchable. I sensed in him a deep well of understanding and a profound wisdom beyond his years. And, he had a special gift—the ability to translate ancient philosophy & dense theory into down-to-earth, real-world lifestyle practices.

That moment was almost two decades ago. And, since that time Adam has mastered his twice-a-day meditation practice; dedicated himself more deeply to sharing the timeless teachings of present moment awareness; taught thousands of people living high-pressure lives to settle into their own stillness; and cultivated a purpose-driven life. Adam is that rare being—both a dedicated student of life and a masterful teacher who walks the talk and embodies the teachings. But, even more profound—is his understanding of exactly where you're at right now and the steps you can take to shift your life from where you are to where you'd like to be.

So, the Timing is perfect—you are ready . . . you have given yourself permission to step into your power; the Message is clear—by connecting to the stillness & silence that rests within, you will make better choices & take your life to the next level; and the Messenger is a brilliant teacher who has opened his heart to guide you to your best expression. All three converge right here . . . right now . . . in this sacred precious present moment. So, I invite you to dip your toe into this magnificent ocean of timeless wisdom with Adam as your guide and to let your transformation unfold. Take a deep breath in . . . connect to that space that rests within . . . and now let it go. The best is yet to come!

—davidji, author of *Sacred Powers: The Five Secrets to Awakening Transformation* (Hay House, 2017)

INTRODUCTION

I've meditated every day for the past twenty-two years. It's the first thing I do every morning and the first thing I do when I come home from work in the evening. Whenever I'm traveling or on vacation, I make sure to carve out time in my schedule to fit meditation in. I guess you could say I have a meditation lifestyle. It's become a fundamental part of each day and it's hard to imagine what my life would be without it.

However, it wasn't always this way. I didn't become a daily meditator overnight. I remember those days before I started a regular meditation practice. Allow me to give you a little back story.

I grew up living in the country, on the outskirts of an old steel town in Western Pennsylvania. My younger brother and I spent much of our formative years playing outside—hiking, exploring a small stream, and wrestling on the front lawn. Our parents, both school teachers, worked hard to keep our little family afloat while instilling in us a profound curiosity of the world and an appreciation for learning. We both developed a love of comic books and science fiction that continues to this day. These two overlapping genres helped to expand my imagination and made me wonder: *Exactly what is possible and what am I capable of?*

In 1980 my mother, a science teacher, introduced our family to the now famous PBS television series *Cosmos*, in which the iconic astrophysicist Carl Sagan showed us the world as we had never seen it before. I was inspired and fascinated by the way science could explain both how the universe worked while also predicting the way everything from house plants to planets behaved.

Despite this inspiration, I often struggled in school. In the classroom, science and mathematics were not my friends. Music and art were much more up my alley. I excelled in band, choir, and theater. I enjoyed performing and seemed to find a little niche that looked like a promising direction for a career. But late in my high school years I was exposed to the work of an artist, philosopher, and actor that had a huge impact on the way I would see the world from that time forward. His name was Bruce Lee.

Bruce's charisma and martial arts skill on the screen drove me to explore his art, known as Jeet Kune Do as well as his unique and revolutionary philosophy. I would learn that his worldview had been informed not only by his own Chinese Taoist and Gung Fu roots, but also by the Zen scholar Alan Watts and Indian Sage-Mystic Jiddu Krishnamurti. As I studied Bruce's teachings, a passion to understand our human potential was ignited within me.

This fascination with Eastern philosophy and martial arts accompanied me when I went off to college in 1987. I officially majored in theater and music, but in my spare time I devoured books and audio programs by Joseph Campbell, Alan Watts, Bruce Lee, Ram Dass, Aldous Huxley, Houston Smith, and countless others. I didn't realize it then, but my study of theater and performance would help to deepen my interest in the subtleties of the human experience. Specifically, I recall attending an acting class that ended up having a significant impact on my life. As part of a regular assignment, I had been asked to perform a monologue in front of my fellow students and our acting coach. Everyone listened attentively to my speech until, right in the middle of my delivery, our teacher began to riddle me with rapid-fire questions as I spoke my lines: *Who are you? What do you want? Why are you here? What is your motivation?* Although I was thrown off by the interruption I was directed to go on with the scene as if nothing was happening. Our coach again repeated the questions (several times) while snapping his fingers in a rhythmic tempo. It was as if he was trying to pull the answers out of my skull by sheer force. I can only imagine that he was disappointed by the blank stare I gave him when my monologue ended, but my coach went on to explain that the purpose behind his questioning was to get me to more deeply embody the role I was playing. It was an exercise meant to help explore my character's motivation, needs, and wants so I could be more realistic in my performance.

Walking back to my dorm room after class, I understood the purpose behind the exercise intellectually, but what struck me were the questions themselves. I realized that not only was I unable to answer those questions about the character I was playing, but deep down I couldn't answer those questions about *myself*. I didn't know who I was, what I wanted, why I was here, or where I was going.

Up until this point, my study of the world's great philosophers and wisdom traditions had been more or less an academic hobby. Yes, I had begun to understand the *theory* behind some of these philosophies, but what I needed now were practical answers to these deep questions. Years later I would learn that questions like this were literally the most profound questions you could ask yourself, and that repeatedly asking, "who am I?" (and the consequent shift in awareness brought on by the deepening answers) could lead to enlightenment. But I'm getting ahead of myself . . .

Through my youth I had been raised in the Protestant Christian tradition, but I didn't feel as if that education was able to give me the answers I sought. So with renewed zeal I intensified my search into some of the world's great "isms"—Buddhism, Taoism, Hinduism, and Confucianism to see how they answered the big questions. World religions fascinated me as much as philosophy and had I not nearly completed all my required courses to earn my theater and music degrees, I probably would have changed my major to something more aligned with my growing passion. It's funny how things work out.

Unfortunately, my ongoing study into the nature of reality was bearing little fruit. In Alan Watt's wonderful book, *The Book on the*

Taboo Against Knowing Who You Are, he exclaims "You are the works!" meaning that *you are the universe*. But deep down, I had no idea or actual experience of what that really meant. Other authors and ideologies suggested similar notions (it's amazing how close the world's great faiths are to each other when you get past their superficial differences), but for some reason the idea wasn't getting through my thick head in a way that resonated with me. Still, I continued to read and explore, dabbling in anything that might take me closer to the deeper understanding I was seeking. From rune stones, to dowsing, to Native American sweat lodges, I was rapidly becoming a New Age poster boy (no doubt to the chagrin of my parents and science-minded brother).

This was also when I first learned about meditation. Several of the books I read extolled the value of meditation for understanding our deeper nature. They all seemed to agree that if one was sincerely trying to know who they were, meditation was the first and most fundamental step on that journey. It sounded good enough for me to try. And try I did, multiple times, seemingly without success. Maybe it was me, or the instruction, or the books or cassettes I was using, but I was just not getting it. I had no real way of knowing if I was doing it right, if something was supposed to happen, or if was just losing my mind. Either way, it didn't stick despite my best efforts. I wanted it to work for me, but sitting alone in my dimly lit dorm room, I knew something was missing. I just didn't know what.

I suppose out of frustration and the need to complete my formal education in order to graduate, I put my philosophical yearnings on the back burner while I attended to my classes and planning for my future outside of college. Those questions still haunted me, but other matters, such as a passing grade in Spanish, demanded my attention.

Upon graduating from college in 1991, I moved to Florida to work in the hospitality industry. I had family in the Florida Keys and both the job and company were a good fit for what I figured would be a two to three year hiatus until I could put myself through graduate school in philosophy or some other deep-thinking field of study. Once I was settled in my new job and not having to study required courses to graduate, I renewed my interest in philosophy, religion, martial arts, and the mystery of the human experience. Fortunately for me, but not for my bank account, I lived within walking distance of a bookstore and during one of my regular visits as I perused the self-help/wellness section, I came across an audiobook with an intriguing title: *Ageless Body, Timeless Mind; The Quantum Alternative to Growing Old*. It was written and read by an author I had never heard of before—Dr. Deepak Chopra.

I listened to this audiobook for the first time as I made my twice-weekly commute to my martial arts class in downtown Orlando. After years of study, reading, and dabbling, as I listened to that tape something shifted in me. Things began to make more sense than they had up until then. I can't say it was like a lightbulb going on for me, but due to Deepak's skill in translating the abstract and esoteric ideas hidden in the world's wisdom traditions (in this case Vedanta and Ayurveda) I began to grasp these concepts at a much deeper level than I had before. I was hooked and had to know more.

I quickly gobbled up more of Deepak's work—*Quantum Healing, Creating Affluence, The Seven Spiritual Laws of Success,* and *Perfect Health*—all of which served to deepen and fill in the gaps in knowledge I had accumulated up to this point. In addition, all of these books praised the power of meditation. Now if this guy, a doctor, was talking about the power of meditation to heal, reverse aging, experience success in our lives, and explore our true nature, I knew I definitely needed to get in on it.

Around this time I must have somehow gotten my name and address on the Chopra Center's mailing list (these were the days before the internet), and one fateful day in 1996 I received an invitational flyer to attend a weekend workshop with Deepak Chopra called *Journey to the Boundless*, during which he would also be teaching meditation. I probably decided in a heartbeat that I would attend. The workshop was being held in Reston, Virginia, a two-day road trip for me, but I didn't care. I was determined to learn to meditate and learn it right.

Some believe there are moments in each life that, if seized, can change the course of that lifetime forever. For me, the weekend at that workshop was such an event. Under the thoughtful and enlightening care of the Chopra Center staff, I successfully learned Primordial Sound Meditation, a technique derived from the ancient Vedic and Yogic traditions of India. Through both lectures and personal instruction, I came to understand the how's and why's of this timeless technique for expanded awareness, fulfillment, and well-being. The impact was huge for me, not only because I had learned the proper way to meditate, but because through meditation I was able to glimpse the answers to the questions that had been haunting me. I was hooked and made the commitment to meditate for the recommended time—twice a day.

While at the workshop, I also attended a separate information session on becoming a meditation instructor. The speaker, a meditation instructor himself, Roger Gabriel, explained that if we enjoyed our own meditation practice, we would enjoy teaching others a hundred times more. It sounded like a good sales pitch and I knew that my coworkers in the hospitality industry would undoubtedly benefit from learning to meditate, but, unfortunately, I didn't have the resources to attend the meditation teacher training program at that time. It would have to wait.

Upon returning from the workshop, my meditation practice began to take off and deliver some wonderful benefits. I felt less stressed, anxious, and emotionally reactive. I felt more grounded, peaceful, and aware. And I began to have a better idea of who I was and what I wanted.

Later that year, I attended a week-long meditation retreat during which I spent six hours a day in meditation. It was an incredible experience that helped me to deepen my practice as well as introduce me to more advanced meditation techniques. These techniques, along with accompanying yoga sessions, helped me to see the world with new eyes. It was a world I wanted to explore even more thoroughly. So in 1999, after volunteering at several Chopra Center events, I decided to move to San Diego, California, in the hopes of working at the Chopra Center in La Jolla.

While the job I was hoping for never materialized, I did have the opportunity to deepen my studies, attend some incredible seminars and workshops, write a book, and hang out at the Chopra Center as much as time allowed. And although I wasn't experiencing a lot of forward momentum in my life during this period, I would later come to recognize the wisdom in John Lennon's oft quoted words, "Time you enjoy wasting is not wasted time."

Nine months later I would move back to Florida and my old job, which soon led me to new opportunities, roles, a wonderful wife, and eventually the finances that allowed me to enroll in the meditation teacher training program I had long hoped for. I studied with a passion I hadn't before experienced. After meditating for a decade, I was thrilled to discover there was so much more to learn about meditation as part of the teacher training program. I devoured the home study materials before attending the week-long certification program in March of 2006.

When I returned to Florida as a newly minted meditation instructor, I once again became acutely aware of how profoundly important this knowledge could be to my friends, family, and coworkers. I began teaching my first classes in our small living room, sharing these teachings with whoever would listen. And to my pleasant surprise, I quickly learned that teaching meditation was indeed, as Roger had promised, even more enjoyable than practicing it myself.

Fast forward a few more years and a few instructor certifications later (Yoga and Ayurvedic Mind-Body Wellness), I began to make it my mission to share meditation with my company on a large scale. I modified the curriculum to be slightly more business-savvy and geared to the needs of busy employees, managers, and executives. I took meditation to them, rather than forcing them to come to it. I learned through experience that when I made meditation accessible and practical in a nonsectarian way, it was more likely to fall on receptive ears in the business world. This approach seemed to work as more employees turned to meditation to help manage stress and improve wellness as well as enhance performance, creativity, and business vibrancy than ever before. Whether in voluntary after-work sessions or at corporate wellness team-building sessions, meditation has been (and continues to be) a powerful tool for transformation both in my life and in the lives of those I have been fortunate enough to teach.

That's my story so far. The story of a curious, confused kid looking for answers to life and its mysteries and how meditation helped him find some of those answers and discover his purpose by sharing it with others.

Now it's your turn. It's your chance to experience what meditation can do for you. That's why I wrote this book. After teaching meditation in both private groups and in large corporations for over a decade I've realized that I might have something unique to say—a way of making meditation accessible in a way it hasn't been before, a way that might just resonate or "click" with *you*.

You might be wondering, if I personally couldn't learn meditation from a book, why would I want to write a book on meditation? The answer is that although I believe meditation instruction is best taught by an experienced teacher in a live setting, I believe that the fundamentals of meditation can be shared in writing. The tricky part lies in being able to answer the student's questions as only an experienced instructor can do. To that end, I'm approaching this book as if I was teaching you in person and addressing many of the questions you (as a new meditator) will have, hopefully before you have them. For those deeper questions or explorations that still persist after the instruction and follow-up explanations, you'll find a list of recommended reading and resources at the end of the book. In that way you will ideally come

INTRODUCTION

away from this book with a thorough, practical, and grounded understanding of meditation.

ABOUT THIS BOOK

I chose to name this book *The Path to Stillness* because in my experience, the practice of meditation is literally, a path to stillness. So many of us are searching, often desperately for some quiet, some respite from the chaotic swirl of daily activity. The modern world is a hectic, turbulent, and unsettled environment. In Ayurveda, India's consciousness-based system of healing, and yoga's sister science of life, we find descriptions of three fundamental principles in nature: *Vata*: the principle of movement; *Pitta*: the principle of metabolism; and *Kapha*: the principle of structure. According to Ayurveda, health, happiness, and fulfillment in life are maintained by keeping these principles in balance and functioning harmoniously. Unfortunately, the world we inhabit is, what in Ayurveda is known as *Vata Deranged*. This is a state of hyperactivity, anxiety, restlessness, lack of focus, instability, and general confusion. With this imbalance of Vata in our environment, daily life can feel like an endless tornado of activity with each of us searching for some way to slow down the merry go round and just *be*, even if for only a few moments.

What *The Path to Stillness* offers is a way to find some stillness, quiet, tranquility, and shelter from the storm of so much physical, mental, and emotional activity. It shows you a well-trodden path that ironically, rather than taking you to some far distant mountain cave, takes you to the deepest source of stillness—within your own awareness. Follow this path and you'll find a well of calm that will never run dry.

I've divided the material in this book into three primary sections.
   1. The first section helps to answer two questions: What is meditation, and how do I do it? In this section we'll look at exactly

what meditation is, where it comes from, myths and misconceptions about it, and how we actually *do* meditation.
2. The second section helps to answer a third question: Why should I bother? This section explores all the amazing benefits of a regular meditation practice on a physical, mental, emotional, and spiritual level.
3. The third section is about building a sustainable meditation practice. Here we'll explore tools to create a fruitful practice as well as delve into techniques to deepen your meditation.

Through both sections I will be giving my own examples and interpretations based upon my years of practice both as a meditator and instructor in the hopes of making the study of meditation fun, interesting, inspiring, and transformative.

I've also done my best to make meditation accessible and down to earth for everyone. One of the challenges faced by the early Western pioneers who traveled to the East in search of these teachings was translating and adapting this knowledge into our contemporary culture. Often a seeker would go to India, Japan, China, or other faraway land to live in ashrams and monasteries, sit with gurus, or apprentice themselves to spiritual masters. Upon returning to the West they would begin sharing the teachings and techniques with eager new students. However, sometimes those teachings and practices had been designed for the *spiritual renunciate*, someone who had isolated themselves from ordinary life in order to dedicate themselves fully to their studies, rather than the layperson or householder. As a result, the techniques and practices may have been too strict, elaborate, complicated, or intense for many people. I believe that in order to take meditation to the masses, it must meet you *where you are*. Not all of us are ready for (or interested in) living in a Zen monastery. But that doesn't mean our lives can't be benefited from the power of meditation taught in a practical, modern, and effective manner. Sometimes the simplest teachings are the most profound, and to that end I've worked diligently to make these teachings available to you, the reader, no matter your background or experience. Plus, as Albert Einstein once said, "If you can't explain it simply, you don't understand it well enough." It is my hope that my background as a meditator and teacher have helped to bring a rather complicated and nuanced subject down to earth in the simplest way possible.

In closing, I want to thank you for taking this journey with me. As someone who has stood where you stand, looking from the outside into the world of meditation, I can understand what you may be feeling—a little uncertain, a little curious, or perhaps hopeful that meditation can help you improve the quality of your life in some way. We all come to the practice of meditation for different reasons and on our own terms. Some are seeking a mental refuge, others a relief from a physical condition or to improve their health. Others may be wrestling with difficult emotions such as grief, depression, or anxiety. Still others may be seeking spiritual answers or expanded states of awareness. Regardless of who you are, know that whatever brought you here is the right reason. In my experience, I've found that people seek the powerful and transformative benefits of meditation when the time is right, and only one person knows when that time is right—you.

I welcome you to the knowledge, the wisdom, and the transformation that awaits on the Path to Stillness.

With gratitude,
Adam Brady

PART 1
WHAT IS MEDITATION, AND HOW DO I DO IT?

CHAPTER 1

WHAT IS MEDITATION?

If you picked up this book, it's probably because at some point you read an article, watched a video, or heard someone describing meditation and it sparked some interest. Maybe you know a little bit about meditation and want to learn more or perhaps you're a total newbie venturing out into undiscovered territory, looking for answers to questions you don't yet realize you have. Regardless, it's safe to say that you probably have *some* inkling of what meditation is. So if I were to ask you to define meditation, what would you say?

Here are some of the common ways people define meditation:

- A way to make your mind quiet
- A feeling of being grounded, centered, and at peace
- A way to let go of stress
- A relaxation technique
- Present-moment awareness
- Reconnecting with your true self
- Silence, stillness, and letting go

These descriptions are a good start, but what I want to do here is give you a solid definition and understanding of exactly what meditation is, what it isn't, and how to navigate your way through some of the myths and misconceptions that surround this timeless practice.

Here's the way I define meditation: A simple and effortless technique that allows us to make contact with the stillness and silence at the core of our being; a way in which we can go beyond the turbulent activity of our minds to a place of pure, unbounded, present-moment awareness.

However, if that's too much of a mouthful, we can distill the essence of meditation down simply to *a way to calm the mind*.

Let's unpack this definition in some detail.

People often believe that meditation is about *forcing* your mind to become quiet. This isn't the best way to think about it, because in reality you can't "make" your mind be quiet. It just doesn't work that way. In the East, the mind is often compared to a monkey jumping from branch to branch, in a state of perpetual motion. If you try to catch the money and hold him down, he'll go bananas (pun intended). The mind behaves in much the same way. If you try to force your mind into stillness by yelling "STOP THINKING" to yourself, you may experience a few seconds of quiet, but before you know it, your mind ramps back up again, more agitated than before. It's been estimated that we have somewhere between 60,000 to 80,000 thoughts a day, so it's not likely that we can simply switch off that torrent through sheer force of will.

However, the mind can settle down naturally and easily if we go about it in the right way. Imagine visiting the Mississippi River, and taking a big glass bell jar and filling it up with river water. What does that water look like? It would be muddy, murky, and impossible to see through clearly. If you screw a cap on the jar and shake it up, does the water get any easier to see through? Of course not; the turbulence of the shaking keeps the water too muddy and cloudy to see through.

But what if you took that jar and placed on a shelf and left it there for a few hours, a day, or even a week? What would the water look like then? Naturally, the sediment and larger particles would settle to the bottom and the water would become clear enough to see through. Our minds work in the same way. If we continue to shake them up

WHAT IS MEDITATION?

with turbulent thoughts, emotions, moods, or memories, our mental environment will reflect those stormy and unsettled conditions. If, on the other hand, we introduce a simple technique that effectively puts our mind on the shelf, so to speak, it too will eventually settle and become calm enough to allow some peace and stillness to creep in. The "monkey mind," preoccupied with a simple task, begins to settle down on its own. Meditation, therefore, is about how we can stop shaking our own jar.

> *Let the waters settle and you will see the moon and the stars mirrored in your own being.*
> —Rumi

Another way to think about meditation is as a method to transcend or "go beyond" the turbulent activity of our mind. For nearly all of our waking time, our minds are in a state of unending activity. What if we could get past or through that activity to a domain of stillness and silence?

Imagine driving down a highway on your way to work. Everything is smooth sailing until you spot a traffic jam ahead. Cars are stacking up and you see the flashing lights of police cars. Fortunately though, you have a navigation app on your phone and it immediately reroutes you to the next exit and out onto a quiet country road away from the mayhem, turbulence, and traffic of the highway. You're able to reach your destination safely and peacefully.

This is what meditation allows us to do. It detours us around the turbulence into a place of deepening stillness, tranquility, and peace. In fact, according to the world's great wisdom traditions, that state of stillness and peace is our true nature and who, at the deepest level, we really are. It's like the ocean; on the surface there could a hurricane blowing, stirring up huge waves, incredible chaos, and churning destruction. But 500 or 800 feet down, on the ocean floor, it's calm and tranquil. This is the nature of your mind—a frenzy of activity on the surface, but pure stillness in its depths. We'll discuss more about this in further chapters, but for now, just know that this domain of calm and silence may not be just a quiet respite from the day's activity, but possibly your soul's hiding place.

Meditation may also be described as the progressive quieting down of the mind into stillness. As it so happens, this is the definition the great sage Patangali gives to explain the practice of yoga in the first line of the *Yoga Sutras*—"Yoga Chitta Vritti Nirodah," meaning yoga is the removal of the fluctuations of the mind. In a way, this means that the practice of meditation can also be considered the fundamental practice of yoga. While this may come as a surprise to some, yoga goes far beyond the stretching, relaxation, and breathing commonly associated with a yoga class. Yoga is a science, a philosophy, a way of life, and a path to liberation from the constricting patterns of thought and metal activity that hold us captive day in and out. The word yoga means *union*—the union of body, mind, spirit, and environment as one. The first step of this union involves the settling of the mind into silence, the essence of which is the practice of meditation.

To take this one step further, meditation is a process that takes you out of the conditioned mind and opens up access to the non-conditioned mind. What exactly does that mean? Well, we all come into this life as a blank canvas, free from restrictions, limitations, and any specific conditioning. As babies we are all free, unbounded, and open to all possibilities. However, as we grow older we begin to have experiences, and those experiences give us feedback on what we think we can and cannot do or become. We acquire constrictions, rules, limiting beliefs, fears, and conditioning that structures the way we think and behave. Good little boys behave this way; good little girls do such and such; you couldn't do that when you grow up; that's not how we behave in this family; you need to follow the rules of your school, church, social structure, etc. Upon reaching adulthood we exist as layer upon layer of conditioning that begins to define what we think we can do and who we are.

Now, for a moment, imagine being able to step outside of that conditioning, to let go of ideas and beliefs you hold about yourself and the world, and simply *be*. Through meditation we access our unconditioned mental state in its original purity and unbounded wonder. Like peeling the layers of an onion, we can, if just for a few minutes, let go of years of conditioning that in many cases, have become the walls of our own self-made prison cell. We can step outside our beliefs and programing to see the world and ourselves in their natural and pristine simplicity.

Lastly, I want to point out the distinctions around the use of the terms *meditation* and *mindfulness*. Over the last several years the word mindfulness has become increasingly popular in the professional and business worlds as a way to describe either a formal practice of meditation or simply the idea of being more present in our day-to-day lives. I think this trend is largely due to an effort to de-spiritualize meditation and make it more appealing as a nonsectarian practice strictly dedicated toward health, well-being, and stress management. Regardless, I've come to view mindfulness primarily as the mental attribute of being fully present in whatever we are doing, non-judgmentally witnessing and accepting each moment just as it is. Much of the time we are not truly present—or we're multitasking—so developing the quality of mindfulness can be of profound benefit in our lives. While mindfulness meditation is a specific technique associated with the Buddhist tradition and contemplative psychotherapy, being mindful simply refers to the act of paying precise, nonjudgmental attention to the details of our experience, allowing them to arise and subside. Meditation on the other hand, is the tool, the practice, or exercise that helps to cultivate mindfulness, both during the practice and throughout our daily activities.

However, outside of the formal sitting meditation practice (and depending on who you talk to), the word mindfulness is somewhat interchangeable with the term meditation. It doesn't matter if you call it *seated meditation* or *mindfulness meditation*, *walking meditation* or *mindful walking*, *eating meditation* or *mindful eating*. In essence, these practices are one and the same. My experience and training has centered on the word meditation, which I see as an umbrella term to describe the vast variety of meditation practices. If you prefer mindfulness, that's fine too. Ultimately, as Bruce Lee once said when referring to his martial art, "It's just a name; don't fuss over it."

This is how I've come to describe and think about meditation. While it's a relatively simple idea, our minds often make it more complicated than it is. I hope some of the subtle nuances I've explained here help to make it slightly easier to grasp. Let's now move on to some of the funny ideas we often hold about this practice.

MYTHS AND MISCONCEPTIONS ABOUT MEDITATION

Over the years the practice of meditation has developed an interesting popular image; some parts of that image are accurate, while others are mistaken, stereotypical, or totally false. I'll admit it, at one time I too was guilty of holding odd or exaggerated assumptions about meditation. For many of us, when we think of meditation an image comes to mind, and in many cases, that image ranges from slightly off the mark to totally ridiculous. Let's take a look at some of the more popular myths and misconceptions surrounding meditation. Hopefully in doing so you'll have a more complete and less intimidating view of this practice.

- **Myth Number 1:** Meditation is difficult. In practice, meditation is pretty simple. As you'll soon see, the technical aspects of meditation are direct, uncomplicated, to the point, and easy. However, our minds have trouble accepting the simplicity of the practice and we end up making it much more difficult than it is. We overthink, analyze, and evaluate the practice, judging and getting ourselves bogged down in expectations and *thinking* about meditation rather than simply *doing* it. We're the ones who make meditation a challenge; however, in and of itself the practice of meditation isn't hard. In fact it's much more challenging to *explain* meditation than it is to just *do* it.

- **Myth Number 2:** Meditation shuts down the thinking process. Many people seem to think that once they start to meditate, a titanium curtain comes down in their mind with a thud, shutting out all outside thoughts. This is rarely the case. Nor is it likely your mind will go blank when you meditate. Meditation slows down the thought traffic in your mind; it may stop for a time, or maybe it won't, but either way, the meditation will still be beneficial. Think of meditation as a way to turn down the volume of your thoughts. They may still be there, just not as loud. Sometimes the volume gets turned down completely, other times it goes down just a little bit. What's more important than the quantity of your thoughts is how you respond to them. Meditation doesn't necessarily make your thoughts go away—it changes how you react to them. It's ultimately about changing your relationship to your thoughts, rather than making them go away.

- **Myth Number 3:** It takes years of dedicated practice to receive any benefits. While several of the long-term benefits of meditation accumulate over time, your mind and body will begin to experience subtle and positive shifts in well-being from the first time you meditate. The benefits of meditation are both immediate and long term. The longer and more regularly you practice, however, the more profound and lasting those changes will become. Meditation is a *practice* in the sense that it's something we do regularly. As with any practice, the more you do it, the better you get at it, and the more powerful the results. Rest assured though, even from the first time out, those benefits will begin to accrue.

- **Myth Number 4:** Meditation is uncomfortable. For many people the word meditation conjures up images of saffron-robed, shaven-headed monks sitting cross legged on a cold wooden monastery floor, mumbling some strange language as they struggle desperately to not fall asleep. Or perhaps it's a vision of a skinny, loin-clothed yogi with his body twisted into a pretzel. These images portray meditation as a terribly uncomfortable and unforgiving experience, both physically and mentally. And while they may be consistent with formal and traditional Eastern meditation practices, here in the West they simply don't work. Being comfortable is an essential ingredient to a successful meditation practice. For the mind to settle into stillness, we need to remove any outside distractions, including putting ourselves into an uncomfortable position. In meditation practice, we always want to be moving toward comfort. If we need to shift or reposition our body, we do that; if we need to scratch an itch, we do; if need to cough or sneeze, we do what we need to be comfortable and not be unnecessarily disturbed by our body. If our meditation isn't comfortable, our bodies will protest and chances are high that we'll end up quitting.
- **Myth Number 5:** Meditation is a religion. Many people who could otherwise benefit from meditation are scared because they incorrectly assume that learning meditation means they are taking part in another religion or violating the doctrines of their faith. This is perhaps one of the most stubborn and challenging misconceptions to dispel, due largely to the fact that meditation arose as a part of many spiritual traditions and is often automatically associated with Buddhism, Hinduism, Taoism, Yoga, Vedanta, or countless other beliefs. However, while meditation is a component of countless spiritual traditions, in and of itself, it is just a

simple mental technique. Practicing meditation doesn't mean you've joined a cult or another religion. In its most basic form meditation is a mental exercise, not unlike any type of physical exercise. A bicep curl has no religious affiliation; it's just a tool used to strengthen your arm. Likewise, meditation doesn't have a religious affiliation; it's just a tool to strengthen your mind, body, and spirit. And as far as this book is concerned, I strive to teach meditation from a nonsectarian approach that can be practiced and embraced by everyone, regardless of their faith or religious beliefs. Plus, many students of meditation find that their practice helps them to have a deeper connection to their faith, whatever it may be.

- **Myth Number 6:** Meditation requires special externals. Often when we think of meditation, we associate the practice with chimes, candles, incense, shawls, beads, robes, cushions, altars, or other external items. It's true, these things can have a place in a meditation practice, but they are *not* required. We spend 90 percent of our waking state with our attention externally focused. Meditation can be referred to as an *inward stroke* —we're directing our attention internally. The external ornaments of a meditation practice may be helpful in creating a comfortable or nurturing environment for meditation, but if you don't want or need those things you'll be able to meditate without them just fine. Furthermore, we don't want a lack of those external items to potentially become a crutch or an excuse for not meditating. Later in the book we'll discuss setting yourself up for a successful meditation practice and talk a little more about these externals, but for now just know that one of the beautiful aspects of this practice is that, as they say, no equipment required. If you can sit down and close your eyes, you can meditate.

- **Myth Number 7:** The I-can't-meditate syndrome. As a meditation teacher, I've heard this excuse more times than I can remember.

People often assume, due to a combination of the previous misconceptions or through some anti-meditation genetic disposition, that meditation is incompatible with them. This myth fosters the notion that meditation is a God-given talent certain individuals are born with while others aren't so lucky. In my experience, this is nonsense. I believe that *everyone* can be taught to meditate and reap the benefits from the practice. I'm guessing that the majority of individuals who believe they can't meditate fall into this trap due to a lack of proper instruction. A good meditation teacher will be able to walk the student through their doubts so they can arrive at a point of comfort and confidence in the practice. Everyone can meditate—even you.

- **Myth Number 8:** "I have too many thoughts!" I imagine 95 percent of people in the modern world would say they have too many thoughts. I've been meditating for twenty-two years and I feel like I have too many thoughts! Having thoughts is part of the human experience, and due to our technological, information-based society it's likely that we have more and faster thoughts than at any time in human history. But that's okay—thoughts are a by-product of life, and no thoughts = flatlining, and we don't want that. Plus, thoughts and meditation aren't mortal enemies. In fact, as you will soon see, thoughts play a necessary role in the meditation process. Don't worry about how many thoughts you have or that they will prevent you from meditating successfully. You can have loads of thoughts every day and still enjoy and benefit from meditation.

- **Myth Number 9:** "I don't have time to meditate." This is a myth/excuse I hear sometimes more often from those I have previously taught to meditate, but it also plagues those new to meditation who just can't imagine making room for a meditation practice in their busy lives. They're often familiar with the multiple benefits of meditation yet they can't seem to find time to practice regularly. In all honesty, this is a matter of priorities more than anything else. Here's the thing—if you have time for Facebook, you have time for meditation; if you have time for the latest reality show, you have time for meditation; if you have time for video games, you have time for meditation. You'll ultimately make time for meditation if you make it a priority in your life. If meditation is just a passing flirtation, chances aren't good that you'll find time for it. But consider that countless, incredibly busy and successful people meditate every day. The only thing that separates them from you is a conscious choice to do this powerful and transformative thing each day. Perhaps meditation is even a key to their success.

In addition, there seems to be a consensus among regular meditators in that, despite giving up fifteen to twenty minutes a day or more to meditation, they feel as if they have more time during the course of their day. As odd as it sounds, this may be due to a couple reasons. First, the sharpening of awareness during meditation makes their non-meditating time more focused, aware, and productive, allowing them to accomplish more in the same amount of time. Second, as we'll discover in an upcoming chapter, when we slip into the stillness between our thoughts, it is a domain of timeless awareness. With practice, we pull some of that timelessness back into our daily lives (more on that later). You'll have time to meditate if you choose to make it an important part of your life—and it will be well worth your time.

Exploring these common myths and misconceptions, I hope you have been able to let go of any notions that might be holding you back from taking the next step into learning meditation. I feel strongly that everyone can meditate and there are no bad meditators, only less efficient ways to learn. The responsibility of conveying the how-to's, the benefits, and subtleties, and nuances of a meditation practice lie with the instructor. In this case, that's me. Meditation works. If you're having difficulty with it, don't blame yourself and think that you're somehow defective, and don't blame the meditation process and think the practice is somehow flawed. Instead, blame me for being a lousy teacher, but don't give up on meditation. Chuck this book out the window and go find another (there are lots of them out there), or go to a class, download an app, or watch a video. Sooner or later, you'll find the method that works for you and eventually understand that meditation is for everyone.

MEDITATION BASICS

Let's now move on to explore the type of meditation we'll be practicing as well as the mechanics of the procedure and why it works the way it does.

The meditation technique we'll be using throughout this book is known as a mantra meditation technique. This practice has its origins in the yoga tradition and is a simple, powerful, and reliable tool to tap into the stillness that's hidden within each of us. *Mantra* is a very specific word that comes from the Sanskrit language, the ancient language of India. And even though it has ancient roots, you may have noticed that this word has begun to creep into our modern vernacular. Perhaps you've heard someone say, "My mantra today is: I am happy, healthy, and strong." However, this is more like an affirmation—a declarative phrase or statement to "make firm" within the mind a desired idea or belief. Affirmations work at the level of the subconscious mind and are used to help re-program negative or limiting beliefs.

A mantra is substantially different than an affirmation. The word mantra consists of two syllables, *man* and *tra*. *Man* means mind; and *tra* means instrument, tool, or vehicle. Therefore, a mantra is a mental instrument used to transcend the mind's regularly turbulent activity. There are countless mantras in the yoga tradition that are comprised of the primordial sounds of nature that can be heard in ocean waves, the wind moving through the trees, a heartbeat, rolling thunder, or even our breath. Mantra captures the essential vibrational quality of the universe in a tangible sound. This is important because the mantra we'll be using has no specific meaning; it is used solely for its vibration.

Whether you notice it or not, the thoughts you think on a daily basis are strung together through the process of association. One thought leads to another, which connects to the next and so forth. If you pay close enough attention, you can retrace the thoughts you have during a given time by noticing how your last thought was tied to the one that came before. Occasionally we have bursts of insight, inspiration, or creativity that seem to "pop" into our awareness out of nowhere, but they too are subtly tied to the thoughts we were thinking earlier. As it relates to this thinking process, the purpose of the mantra is to momentarily interrupt the thought traffic and break the cycle of association to the next thought.

Think of the mantra like a speed bump for your mind. Close to my home there's a country road about five miles long that connects two larger highways. While the road is paved, it has speed bumps covering its surface roughly every 500 yards. As you might imagine, as soon as you're able to pick up any speed in your car, you hit a speed bump and have to slow back down. The speed bumps effectively govern the speed the cars can travel on that roadway.

In much the same way, a mantra governs and slows down the speed of your mental traffic, disturbing the continuity of the thought-stream, and temporarily weakening its grasp on the mind.

Since it has no meaning, the mantra also prevents the mind from forming an association to a similar thought. There are mantras that have a specific meaning that can be used to transcend; however, a meaning-based mantra only makes the process more challenging. For example, if I chose to use the mantra, "Om Cherry Cheese Danish," through repetition, my mind might eventually become quieter and more settled. But sooner or later my attention may drift to the meaning of the word cherry, cheese, or danish and before I know it, I'm visualizing a pastry shop or my mother's cherry pie, and the thought-stream has begun to flow again. A mantra without meaning makes this experience less likely.

In this way the mantra is like an anti-adhesive for the mind. Our thoughts can be "sticky;" ask anyone who suffers from anxiety or who might be waiting on some important news. One tiny thought globs onto other similar thoughts and before you know it, like a pebble rolling down a snowbank, that singular thought has caused an unstoppable cascade of worry, doubt, or fear.

Consider this all-too-familiar situation: you visit the doctor for a physical and as part of your checkup your physician wants to run a few routine tests. The tests are performed and you are told the results will be available in two weeks. Home you go to wait for the news. After a day or two you begin to wonder about the results. A few more days pass and you're becoming a little worried. After a week you've become increasingly anxious and begin thinking something could be seriously wrong. By the time the doctor calls you at the end of the two weeks to tell you everything is fine, you've already made funeral arrangements.

This is how our thoughts stick to each other. The mantra is like Goo-Gone for your mind; it helps to prevent the thoughts from bunching and clinging together, reducing their stickiness, and allowing them to flow with less resistance.

What's happening is this: we easily and gently repeat the mantra silently to ourselves, and as we do thoughts arise. But rather than getting pulled into their meaning or substance, we effortlessly guide our awareness back to the mantra. Again and again this happens, with our sole activity being to gently return our attention to the mantra.

In the most basic sense, the mechanics of this process consists of just two steps:

1. Becoming aware or noticing that your attention has drifted away from the mantra
2. Bringing your attention back to it

That's it. Seriously. This simple exercise of realizing that you are no longer repeating the mantra and then coming back to it is the essence of the practice. Catch and release. It's like when you are trying to take a photograph of a toddler. You position them right where you want them to be, try to get them to smile, and just as you're about to snap the picture, they move or crawl off after something shiny. You reposition them and try again. They crawl off again. Rinse and repeat. It's the same with meditation. Beginners can sometimes become frustrated because it's suddenly painfully apparent just how slippery their minds are. But it's all part of the process and it happens to *everyone*.

As I mentioned in the introduction, I study and train in a martial art called Jeet Kune Do. Jeet Kune Do was founded by Bruce Lee and the name translates as "the way of the intercepting hand or foot." In the simplest terms, it means that you are beating your opponent to the punch. Using a combination of highly developed attributes such as speed, timing, coordination, body mechanics, and line familiarization you catch your opponent's movement with your own and hit him before he hits you. In the context of meditation however, to Jeet can refer to catching or intercepting *your thoughts*.

To go a little deeper, in the philosophy of the martial arts, there are generally three times when you can strike your opponent:

1. *Before* his movement
2. *During* his movement
3. *After* his movement

The same timing applies as we meditate. In the beginning we may not catch ourselves thinking a thought until it is well developed and spinning off with a mind of its own, so to speak. With more practice and awareness, we may notice the thought as it unfolds, but before it has sunk deep roots in our mind. Ultimately, we may learn to perceive the impulse of a thought before it manifests into expression.

In the beginning this takes practice and patience. But as time goes on you become more adept at intercepting your mind's tendency to drift away. It still happens, but the interval eventually begins to grow smaller. You notice just as your mind begins to wander and you pull it back, again and again.

Through this process, as the thoughts and mantra interact, a strange thing starts to happen—both thoughts and mantra begin to grow fainter, softer, and less tangible. In effect, the thoughts and mantra start to wear each other away as if by friction of rubbing up against each other.

Here's another way to think about it: imagine you've decided to build a beautiful wooden dining room table. You head to your local hardware or home supply store and buy the raw lumber for your project, bring it home, and then measure, cut, nail, and glue everything together. Now that you have the unfinished wood assembled, your next task is to sand the surface so it's nice and smooth. To do this, you use a coarse sandpaper to buff out the roughest spots. In the process the coarse sandpaper wears out, so you switch to a finer grade of paper and continue sanding. As this procedure goes on, the sandpaper gets finer and the table gets smoother until, eventually, the table is perfectly smooth, almost frictionless, allowing your polishing cloth to effortlessly slide across the surface.

This is much the same way the mantra and thought interact. The mantra rubs against the thought and both components become increasingly lighter, softer, and more abstract. In other words, the firm and concrete nature of our day-to-day thinking starts to become fainter and less rigid. Occasionally during this process the thoughts and mantra disappear entirely, allowing the pure stillness beneath our mental activity to emerge.

WHAT IS MEDITATION?

Such is the back and forth nature of thoughts and mantra. I often visualize this interaction through the infinity symbol (∞); the thought leads to mantra and mantra cycles back to thought, repeating endlessly throughout the meditation. Thoughts and mantra work together to their eventual dissolution, at which point we experience pure present-moment awareness. We don't *try* to make this happen through force or effort, which would be shaking the jar of river water we mentioned earlier. Rather, through this gentle and effortless process, we put the jar on the shelf and let the mind settle into stillness of its own accord.

SO-HUM MEDITATION PRACTICE

Now that you understand the mechanics of how this meditation technique works, it's time for you to experience it firsthand. What follows are simple instructions that will help you tap into the stillness that resides within you. I recommend reading through them several times so that you fully understand and grasp the procedure before you begin. Once you're familiar with this process, I suggest starting out with a ten-minute meditation test drive. Simply follow the instructions and take note of how you feel—mentally and physically—before and after you meditate. Enjoy!

- Sit comfortably where you will not be disturbed and close your eyes.
- For a few minutes simply observe the inflow and outflow of your breath. Observe the sensation of air as it enters your nostrils, slowly fills your lungs, pauses briefly, and flows back out. Don't try to force or control your breath; simply let it be natural and easy.
- On your next breath, inhale through your nose while silently thinking the word *So*.
- Exhale slowly through your nose while thinking the word *Hum*.

- Allow your breathing to flow easily, silently repeating, *so . . . hum . . .* with each inflow and outflow of your breath. *So* on the inhale, *hum* on the exhale. There is no particular speed, rhythm, or pitch. Just think the mantra easily, effortlessly.
- Whenever your attention drifts to thoughts in your mind, sounds in your environment, or sensations in your body, innocently and without judgment come back to your breath and the sound of the mantra. Let go of any thoughts passively and gently.
- Continue this process for ten to twenty minutes with an attitude of effortless simplicity.
- When the time is up, sit with your eyes closed for a couple of minutes before resuming your daily activity.

This is the so-hum mantra meditation practice that we will be returning to throughout this book. It is a simple, reliable, comfortable, and powerfully effective technique to bring about healing and transformation at all levels of our being—physical, mental, emotional, and spiritual.

Before continuing on to the next chapter, I would recommend practicing this technique three to four more times over one or two days. If you're excited about what's to come, by all means read on. However, the purpose behind you practicing the technique before proceeding further is simply to allow you the opportunity to gather some meditation experience. In the back of this book, you'll find a Meditation Journal that provides some space for you to log your first few meditations. In it you can list where you meditated, for how long, and what you experienced during the meditation. While we don't usually record our meditations, in the beginning, it's a good way to keep track of your experiences. In addition, if you become a long-term meditator, in the future you'll be able to look back fondly and reflect on how those first meditations paved the way for your ongoing practice.

In the chapter that follows we'll be looking specifically at the types of experience you may have during meditation. Therefore, if you've practiced the technique a few times, you'll likely have had some of those experiences, which will lend insight and context to the discussion.

> *The gift of learning to meditate is the greatest gift you can give yourself in this lifetime.*
> —Sogyal Rinpoche, Tibetan Buddhist Teacher

CHAPTER 2

WHAT YOU CAN EXPECT

Now that you've had the opportunity to meditate a few times, you might have a few questions floating through your mind: Am I doing this right? Is something special supposed to happen? Is this so-hum thing all there is?

All of these questions are perfectly normal when you first begin to meditate. If you're new to meditation, it's only natural for you to be a little uncertain and unsure of yourself and the practice in the beginning. Good news: that uncertainty is exactly what this chapter is meant to address. In the sections that follow we'll explore the experiences you can have during meditation along with some expectations and values of the practice. Typically, we don't spend a lot of time discussing these aspects of meditation, but that's exactly what we're going to do here. Once you thoroughly understand how the practice works and the experiences you can expect, your intellect will hopefully be satisfied enough to accept the theory so you can simply enjoy the practice without dwelling on the how's and why's. With that said, let's look at the experiences you may have during meditation.

TYPES OF EXPERIENCES DURING MEDITATION

In this style of mantra meditation, there are typically only four specific experiences you may have when you meditate. Most of these are straightforward and simple to grasp as they happen to us as meditators on a regular basis. Once you see that each of these four options is a normal part of the practice, you'll understand that no matter which happen to you, you're meditating correctly.

1. **Mantra awareness.** There are times during meditation that your attention will be completely absorbed with the repetition of the mantra. This is not surprising for a few reasons. First, for most of us, the mantra so-hum is a unique sound, possibly unlike other sounds that we're accustomed to. This may make it more noticeable or cause it to stand out in your awareness. Second, the act of repeating a specific sound over and over may also be a distinctive experience that causes your attention to lock-in on that repetitive phrase more so than other thoughts. But no matter the reason, this is a regular experience during our practice. We may simply experience all mantra, all the time.

    This is a good time to discuss a few additional details regarding the use of the mantra. Specifically, as we silently think the mantra to ourselves, it is an effortless repetition. We are not concentrating, struggling, or forcing the mantra into our awareness. In fact, the experience is more like listening for the mantra than deliberately articulating it in our mind. Nor are we trying to drown out other thoughts with the mantra. It's not a matter of turning up the internal volume of the mantra to overwhelm or bury our regular thinking process. The mantra isn't meant to be the bouncer of your mind, deliberately preventing the unwelcome thoughts from getting in. Rather, the mantra is like a whisper of a vibration passing through your awareness, soft and gentle. As one of my teachers Davidji likes to say: "The repetition of the mantra is effortless, like mist rising off a lake at dawn. Any more effort and you're working way too hard."

    Furthermore, the mantra has no set speed, rhythm, or pitch. It may get faster or slower, the syllabic emphasis may switch from *so* to *hum* and back again, or the mantra may change, becoming distorted or strange in some way. I sometimes call this "Frankenstein-ing" the mantra. All of these things are normal. Allow them to happen without trying to control the mantra or force it in any way. Permit it to do whatever it's going to do. If the mantra dissolves completely and becomes totally unrecognizable, simply bring it back into your awareness with slightly more attention and continue the practice. The mantra may also become uncoupled from the breath. If so, you may either gently realign it with your breathing cycles or simply continue to repeat it separately—whichever is more comfortable for you at the time.

2. **Lots of thoughts.** Chances are that during your meditation practice you experienced thoughts, maybe a lot of thoughts. As was touched upon in the previous chapter, thoughts are part of the process, so don't be surprised or alarmed when they frequently show up during your meditation. Thinking thoughts is what our mind does; those thoughts will take myriad forms during meditation. It may even seem as if your thoughts are more vivid or powerful while you are meditating. This only makes sense when you consider that for most of us, we rarely turn our attention within and confront our thoughts face to face. Most of the time our thoughts operate in the background of our awareness, much like the programming language of a computer. Once we begin to meditate, however, we become powerfully aware of the quality of our thoughts, their content, and their illusive, frenetic behavior.

These thoughts will come in all shapes and sizes. You may experience memories, desires, fantasies, moods, emotions. Physical sensations in your body will register as thoughts as will visual sensations in the form of lights or colors, sounds in the environment, or even subtle mental sounds that seem to be as real as external sounds. As the repository of sensory experiences, our mind has the potential to contain all these types of thoughts and more. Most thoughts will fall into one of two broad categories: 1) a future thought in the form of a desire or anticipation or 2) a past thought in the form or a memory or worry. Regardless of their content though, we treat all thoughts the same way; we simply bring our attention back to the mantra.

It helps to know that our thoughts can be slippery and may be subverted by the ego to pull you away from the meditation practice. The ego, our false sense of self, is not a fan of your desire to meditate and will present you with convincing arguments for abandoning the meditation. It will repeatedly assault you with reasons why each thought is incredibly important and demands your full attention, now. Without going into a detailed description of the ego's motives for its compulsion for you to put off your meditation, simply recognize the ego's game early on and politely tell it to sit down and be quiet for a while as you meditate.

Our goal is to treat even the most seemingly important and significant thoughts in the same manner as every other thought. During meditation it's not unheard of to have inspirations or bursts of creative insight pop into your awareness. These thoughts seem so vital and real that we often feel compelled to stop meditating to write them down or delve into them deeper. You might have an insight into a new product, or an idea for a book; you may feel a unique physical sensation or as if you are experiencing another state of consciousness. These are all to be treated as you would any other thought. Even if in your mind's eye you see a golden Buddha levitating on a flying carpet surrounded by choirs of angels—just come back to the mantra. The idea is to let go of *all* thoughts, no matter how amazing, sacred, or holy, as they are all just constructs of your mind.

No different are negative thoughts, mental states, or moods. I often hear students expressing frustration over having too many thoughts during meditation. But then I ask: What is frustration? Is it not simply another thought? Or sometimes the process of repeating the mantra can feel so uneventful, ho-hum, or meh. But boredom, just like frustration, is merely another thought. Seen this way any difficult mental state is simply a thought that we can let go of as we turn our attention back to the mantra, if only for the time we are meditating. If our thoughts are truly that important or earth-shattering, they will still be there when we complete our meditation.

It can be helpful to know that many meditative and contemplative traditions liken the practice of meditation to watching clouds drifting across the sky. When we look at the sky we often study the clouds, comparing them to familiar shapes or objects, but the purpose was to watch the *sky*, not to get caught up in each cloud as it passes before us. In the same way we don't dwell on the thoughts as they drift through our awareness, we allow them to pass without losing ourselves in the process. In this way, the mantra, which is just another thought itself, is like the often-seen police officer in television and films who says, "Please move along folks, nothing to see here."

Let me pause here briefly to point out that although meditation is sometimes referred to as a *contemplative* practice, in this style of meditation it is not our intention to contemplate anything. We're deliberately *not* trying to reflect, ruminate, sleuth-out, or excavate the contents of our thought-stream. All those activities shake the jar of our consciousness rather than allow it to settle. It's not the goal of this type of practice to practice introspection, unearth past traumas, probe into our childhoods, plumb the depths of our past choices, or change self-destructive behaviors. This is not to say that the expanded awareness created by meditation won't provide insight into such things; we just don't do it *during the practice itself*. In this technique, meditation isn't a way to "work on yourself." There are contemplative practices that do just that, but in this simple technique, we allow the stillness within to become the catalyst for transformation (more on that in upcoming chapters).

Sometimes after having a particularly striking thought (i.e., of a friend or relative who you haven't spoken to in years, a frightening image, or a powerful surge of emotion), you may wonder, "What does that mean?" The short answer is, it doesn't necessarily mean anything. Lots of thoughts often simply mean that you're releasing a lot of stress. This is a natural process. As our system settles down during meditation our mind will often take the opportunity to download and unspool excess mental "stuff" that has been stored away within us. Just allow this to happen and avoid the temptation to look for a meaning, even in the most compelling thoughts or images.

3. **Sleep.** Sometimes during meditation your body and mind become so relaxed that you drift off to sleep. This is nothing to be ashamed of or worried about. Often, when I ask my students if anyone has experienced this during meditation, I get a collection of guilty smiles as they admit that they have nodded off. But let's be honest, we live in a profoundly stressed, deeply fatigued, and overworked society. Most of us, if given the chance to sit down, breathe deep, and close our eyes for a few minutes, will naturally fall asleep. So don't feel bad if this happens to you now and again.

With that said, however, it's important to point out that meditation and sleep aren't the same thing. Meditation is known as *restful awareness*, a state in which your body is extremely relaxed, but your mind is still awake and aware. Sleep, on the other hand is *restful dullness*, during which the body is similarly resting and relaxed, but there is much less awareness, so much so that we refer to it as being unconscious. Both meditation and sleep are good and healing for your body and mind, but not in the same ways.

Falling asleep during meditation happens from time to time. It's nothing to be concerned about. Perhaps it's due to the release of large amounts of stress from your system. Maybe you stayed up too late the night before or just had a large meal (incidentally, consuming even as little as one serving of alcohol prior to meditation will often guarantee naptime during meditation). Other times it was just what your mind and body needed at the time. Regardless of why it happens, don't get hung up on it. If you become aware that you were sleeping (usually because you feel heavy or dull), finish whatever time remains of your meditation. Even if you sleep through your entire meditation, try to finish with a few minutes of meditation afterward to preserve the clarity of the meditation.

Occasionally falling asleep just means that you're tired. However, if you find that you fall asleep nearly every time you meditate, it means that you have too much fatigue in your system and you should take steps to bring more balance into your life. Are you getting enough sleep? Are you working too much or too hard? Are you sick or suffering from chronic stress? If any of these are the case, take the time to adjust your schedule or make the lifestyle changes necessary to bring yourself back into a state of balance. Once that balance has returned, staying awake during meditation won't be a challenge. A quick side note about sleep—recent studies have repeatedly shown the vital importance of getting enough sleep each night. A host of health conditions—such as accelerated aging, heart disease, high blood pressure, stroke, Alzheimer's disease, weight gain, lowered sex drive, and diabetes—have been associated with a lack of sleep.

Make sure you get your zzz's each night; your body will thank you for it.

Lastly, meditation is not meant to be a sleep aid. It's true that regular meditation can help regulate your sleeping patterns and may help to reduce insomnia, but I don't recommend using it as a tool to fall asleep. While some of my students have told me they like to meditate right before bed and take advantage of the resulting mental calm and slide right into bed for the night, others have had the exact opposite experience. For some, meditation energizes the system and leaves you feeling wide awake and recharged. Rather than using meditation to fall asleep at night, I would suggest making meditation a regular practice during your waking hours and allow the resulting physiological balance to harmonize and normalize your sleeping patterns spontaneously.

4. **Pure awareness.** Finally, you may have the experience in which there is no mantra, there are no thoughts, and you aren't sleeping. This is the state of pure awareness; not awareness of anything in particular, just awareness itself. This is also known as transcending or slipping into the gap between our thoughts. The Sanskrit name for this state is *atma darshan*, which means "glimpsing the soul."

Of all the experiences we can have during meditation, pure awareness may be the one we're the least familiar with. However, we are entering this gap between our thoughts all the time; it's just so brief that we don't realize it during our daily activity. Through meditation though, this experience becomes more pronounced; the gap expands and we find ourselves in the field of pure stillness, unbounded peace, and infinite possibilities.

There are a few unique qualities of the state of pure awareness that are important to point out. First, you won't become aware of it until after it has happened. This is because you need your thoughts to take note of the experience, and if you're thinking "Oh, I'm in the gap," you're not; because you're *thinking thoughts about being in the gap* rather than just being in it. But, if you have a realization that you're experiencing pure awareness, it's probably because you may have just been there (even though it's not a location). This experience can be summed up in the statement, "Here I am, wasn't I?"

Second, while you're experiencing pure awareness, you'll have no sensation of the passage of time or what is known as temporal discontinuity. Why would this be the case? Well, consider an average day—you wake up, go to the bathroom, shower, have breakfast, head to work, have lunch, work through the afternoon, head home, have dinner, wind down, and eventually head to bed. That timeline of experiences is recorded with a myriad of thoughts—little markers that identify when each experience took place during your day. Now, add a meditation session into your timeline during which you slipped into the gap; for a brief period there were no thoughts. What happens? For a fleeting moment, your timeline is interrupted and time has seemed to stop because there were no thoughts to register any experiences. The first few times this happens it can feel slightly odd, not unlike the sensation of coming out from under anesthesia—you feel as if time has passed, but you have no recollection of what took place. With regular practice though, this experience will begin to feel more and more natural until eventually your mind registers it as a normal part of meditation.

Third, the experience of pure awareness will happen spontaneously. It can't be forced. Sometimes it's brief and hardly noticeable; other times it's more pronounced and is accompanied by a feeling of lightness or expansion. There are meditations when you tap into the gap and feel as if you were lightly "misted" with that stillness. On other occasions you come back with an entire tanker truck of pure awareness in tow. Regardless, the visits to the gap happen without any force or effort on your part. You can't control when, where, or for how long the experience will last, so don't try. Just let go knowing it will show up naturally and effortlessly.

Lastly, the state of pure awareness or the gap isn't a limbo in which you can get lost or stuck. It may sound strange, but to some, this is a legitimate concern. What if when we enter the gap we end up tumbling down an infinite rabbit hole without any thoughts, time, or space to a realm of pure nothingness? Without a link or tether back to the here and now, what's to stop us from slipping into the gap and winking out of existence entirely? Fortunately, we do have a tether to the domain of time and space—that tether is our body. For while our mind seeks expansion into stillness and deeper awareness, our body remains firmly rooted in the here and now. And as relaxed as it will become during meditation, sooner or later, even during the deepest meditation, there will be some sensation—a twitch, a tickle, sneeze, or sound in the environment—that will register as a thought and pull our mind back into activity. In this way, our mind and body is a perfectly matched pair—while one expands toward infinity, the other stays anchored in the material world.

These are the four fundamental experiences you may have during your meditation practice. They are all normal and will become more familiar as you continue to practice. Ultimately, the only real difference between a veteran meditator and a new meditator is that the veteran has become accustomed to these four experiences and allows any or all of them to happen without judgment.

Rest assured that meditation is always healing and that your body takes exactly what it needs from your practice. It doesn't matter if you experience mantra awareness, lots of thoughts, sleep, or the gap; your experiences during meditation are the result of what your physiology and mind/body need at the time. As long as you are meditating comfortably and effortlessly, the experiences you have are the right ones for you. Therefore, *there is no such thing as a bad meditation*. The only way you can fail at meditation is by not doing it.

THE MIND-BODY CONNECTION AND THE PHYSIOLOGY OF STRESS RELEASE

Now let's take a brief look at the incredible way in which our minds and bodies interact so we may better understand how this connection plays into our experiences during meditation. To do so, it helps to recognize that the concept of the mind-body connection or mind-body wellness goes back thousands of years. Ancient traditions of healing such as the Indian system of Ayurveda, Traditional Chinese Medicine, or other indigenous forms of wellness at their root had the fundamental understanding that the mind and body weren't separate components of a person, but rather part of an integrated whole. To our ancestors, this intrinsic connection was self-evident. Unfortunately, in more modern times, we seem to have to have lost touch with our more holistic nature. Fortunately, science has recently begun to rediscover this fascinating realm.

Over the last several decades pioneers in mind-body research such as Herbert Benson MD; Dr. Wilder Penfield MD; Candice Pert, PhD; Bruce Lipton, PhD; Rudolph Tanzi, PhD; Deepak Chopra, MD; and Rupert Sheldrake, PhD, have explored the mechanisms behind the mind-body connection. This research has helped to deeply expand our understanding in fields such as endocrinology, psychoneuroimmunology, epigenetics, and neuroscience. And although the study of the mind-body connection is far from complete and will undoubtedly lead to further discoveries, one conclusion seems to be clear—the mind and body aren't a duality, or two separate things; instead, mind and body are a *unified whole*. Modern science seems to be validating what the ancient wisdom and healing traditions have asserted for thousands of years: *there is no separation between mind and body*. They are deeply interconnected parts of the same thing.

Why does this matter for our discussion on meditation? Well, if mind and body are intertwined, then what affects one can potentially affect the other. In layman's terms, the activity of your mind is being communicated to every cell in your body. There is a constant information exchange taking place in which mind and body are sharing enormous amounts of information in an unending feedback loop. For example, let's say you're watching a comedy movie that you perceive as funny (mind). This perception in turn causes you to burst out in laughter (body). The experience of laughter then triggers a signal to your brain through electro-chemical messenger molecules that registers as a good-feeling emotion, perhaps happiness or joy. This cycle is an ongoing process that allows your mind and body to not only perpetually eavesdrop on each other, but to react to the new information that is being received.

Now, imagine that you have just begun to meditate. The repetition of your mantra begins to settle your mind, which simultaneously triggers deep relaxation in your body. Often, as your mind continues to quieten, blocked energy or bodily tension is spontaneously released from your physiology. This release may cause a muscle to loosen or momentarily twitch as the energy begins to flow once again. Speaking from experience, there have been several times during meditation that despite having stretched or relaxed completely prior to beginning my practice, my body continued to gel or shake off tension I was unaware I was holding onto thanks to the quieting of my mental turbulence.

In a similar manner, the release of physical stress in your body may trigger an increase in your mental activity. This interaction between mind and body isn't necessarily directly correlated. In other words, if while noticing the relaxation of your tight neck muscles you begin thinking about the argument you had with your coworker yesterday, it doesn't necessarily mean that the two are related or that your coworker is a pain in the neck. It's not a direct one-for-one relationship. And for that matter, what's causing your mental or physical activity *doesn't really matter*. The increased movement in mind or body is often just an indicator that stress is being released. Simply remember that it's all part of the mechanics of tension dissolving and your system returning to a deeper state of balance. As these experiences are taking place, our objective remains the same: effortlessly and comfortably bring our attention back to the mantra. Your body and mind will take care of themselves.

EXPECTATIONS DURING MEDITATION

What about having expectations during meditation? Simply put, don't have any. Now that you understand the four primary experiences you may have during your meditation practice, and since there is no one "right" experience to have due to your physiology taking away from the meditation exactly what it needs at the time, having specific expectations can be more of a hindrance to your practice than an asset. Commit yourself to letting go of any attachment to a particular result. Any expectation you have will ultimately slow you down in your practice of meditation. If, for example, you meditate and have a deep and profound experience of the gap (which sooner or later you will), you might think that every meditation will be the same and expect a repeat performance the next time you meditate. When your next meditation is different, as it most likely will be, you may become frustrated and upset that you couldn't duplicate the experience.

There is no agenda in meditation. This probably sounds like a paradoxical idea in that most people choose to meditate in the hopes of receiving one or more of its wonderful benefits. This is, of course, a good thing and the benefits will begin to accrue from the very first meditation. However, during the practice itself we're not trying to get anywhere or accomplish something in particular. We simply follow the steps of the practice and just meditate for the sake of meditating. In our modern world of to-do lists and action items, this notion undoubtedly seems to be both foreign and an incredible waste of time. Sitting still and doing nothing goes against almost everything we've come to believe about being successful and productive, yet it is the doorway to an entirely new level of life skill, performance, and wellness potential. Meditation is the act of letting go of the need to do something and allowing yourself to simply *be*.

Nor are we searching for special effects during our meditation. Film and television often romanticize meditation as a supernormal or science-fiction-y type of experience. We can sometimes fall into the trap of thinking that meditation will lead to extrasensory powers, levitation, precognition, or other fantastic abilities. While I won't discount that such things may be possible, we don't want to get caught up chasing an unrealistic outcome of our practice. Maybe during meditation you have some far-out, awareness-expanding insight, trippy physical sensation, or vision that looks or feels like it was right out of a science fiction blockbuster. Maybe you don't. Once again, any experience you have is a result of what your mind and body need at the time.

Likewise, avoid making the gap the goal. It can be easy to think that pure consciousness is the ultimate "touchdown" of our meditation practice. After all, it sounds so enticing—no thoughts, no mantra, no sensation of time, etc. But attachment to the gap is a barrier that can prevent you from experiencing it, even when that's what your mind and body really need. When you're preoccupied with wondering if and when you'll tap into pure stillness, you're actually trapping your awareness firmly at the level of your thinking mind. Don't be a gap hunter; instead, allow it to find you.

It's also important to be easy and innocent with yourself. Let go of judgment and comparison. Allow each meditation to be a new experience and approach it as if you were doing it for the first time. Each meditation is a unique experience unto itself. Just like a snowflake, there are no two identical meditations. Give your meditation permission to be whatever it chooses.

Remember, as we mentioned earlier, meditation itself is simple and easy to do; it's the overthinking and over-intellectualizing that makes the practice much more difficult than it needs to be. If at any point it feels strained or forced or if your mind is swirling in questions or analysis, pause, take a deep breath, and come back to the practice more gently. Meditation is a natural process, like the sediment settling in our jar of river water. It can't be rushed or forced. Be patient, allow the mind to clear naturally, and eventually you'll begin to glimpse the stillness within.

THE VALUE OF MEDITATION

As odd as it may sound, the tangible and measurable value of meditation lies not during the practice itself. Indeed, the time spent in meditation is comfortable, deeply relaxing, and enjoyable. It's the other twenty-three hours* of your day in which the real magic occurs. To see how well your meditation is working, look for the changes in your life.

* Based upon two, thirty-minute meditations per day.

- Do you feel a greater sense of personal calm?
- Are you more relaxed?
- Do you notice less emotional reactivity?
- Are you less anxious?
- Do you feel happier?

All of these are clues that meditation is having a positive effect on your life. In the chapters that follow, we'll explore the specific benefits that you may begin to notice, but for now just begin to note any general improvements in the overall quality of your life. Through meditation the experience of stillness is brought back into your life and begins to infuse every level of your being.

These changes will happen comfortably, spontaneously, and in a way that is natural for you. Don't worry if you don't notice any difference right away; some people experience an immediate shift, while it may take more time for others. Sometimes friends or family may notice a change before you do. Since you spend every day with yourself, you may not recognize the subtle changes that are taking place. An outside observer, however, might pick up on something new about you and may ask what you've been doing differently. Regardless, know that as long as you are meditating regularly the benefits will continue to grow, and it is in the experience of your non-meditating life that those benefits will be most noticeable.

Having gone through the intellectual exercise of exploring the specific details and experiences we may have during meditation, we can now let them go. We don't want to spend our time analyzing our meditation; talking or thinking about meditation is not the same as doing it. Continue to practice regularly and allow the results and benefits to flow effortlessly into your life.

Once again, remember: Keep calm, and come back to the mantra.

> *Flow with whatever is happening*
> *and let your mind be free.*
> —Chuang Tzu

CHAPTER 3

THE FOUR PILLARS OF MEDITATION

As you'll see in the chapters that follow, the specific physical, mental, emotional, and spiritual benefits of meditation are numerous. However, before we dig into those details, I'd like to briefly address what I call the four pillars of a meditation practice. Rather than specific benefits, these four qualities are both a means and an end of meditation. They are inherent in the overall experience of meditation while at the same time being some of its most rewarding results. Think of the pillars like the legs of a table, each working together to support the entire practice.

The first pillar of meditation is *self-discipline*. Any activity that we repeatedly practice with sincerity and regularity helps to develop self-discipline. It represents the ability to stick to your commitments and follow through on your intentions. Like going to the gym, the regular practice of meditation is an exercise in building mental muscle that grows stronger with use. Meditation requires a certain degree of self-discipline and simultaneously strengthens it.

One of the fundamental aspects of self-discipline is the ability to postpone short term gratification for long-term fulfillment. When we sit down to meditate, we know that some of the benefits are immediate and noticeable; however, many are cumulative and may take time to experience. Rather than reaching for the lowest hanging fruit, self-discipline helps us to continue our practice so we may reap the greater benefit in the long run.

You may be saying, "But I don't have any self-discipline." That's okay. Just take it one meditation at a time. With time and regular practice self-discipline will grow and become self-sustaining. As we'll discuss in Chapter 8, once established, a positive meditation habit can become an internal set point that operates like an autopilot without needing too much effort to maintain.

Self-discipline also helps us:

- Persevere
- Endure hardship
- Persist in the face of challenges and setbacks
- Keep trying until we succeed

This is not to imply that we're beating ourselves into submission or that we become our own mental drill sergeant that inflicts unnecessary suffering upon itself. Rather, the cultivation of self-discipline as it relates to meditation is simply the willingness and ability to keep on keeping on.

When we meditate, we are disciplining the mind by bringing it back to the mantra again and again. We are using a gentle, yet firm hand to return the mind to the focus of our attention. This can feel challenging in the beginning, primarily because for many of us, meditation represents the first time we've ever tried to direct our mental activity. But the more we do it, the better we become at managing our mind rather than simply being along for the ride. With regular practice, we begin to realize that the reward of self-discipline is greater self-discipline.

The second pillar of meditation is *concentration*. Concentration is the ability to hold our mental focus on one thing without allowing it to be pulled away. It is the action or power of centered awareness on the task at hand. It is one of life's most universal tools and improves the quality of virtually any activity we engage in.

Concentration can be considered somewhat of a prerequisite for meditation—not in a laser-locked, stay on target, block out all other stimulus manner, but rather a clear intention to hold our attention on one thing for a period of time. Remember that repetition of the mantra shouldn't involve force, struggle, or effort. There is, however, a softer, more relaxed quality of concentration that is what allows us to keep our attention on the mantra. If this gentle, yet firm quality of concentration wasn't present, we wouldn't be able to get through five minutes of daily activity without chasing after something shiny. That mental persistence is what allows the meditative process to unfold. We all have it to some degree and meditation helps it grow stronger.

If you recall the concept of *Jeet* from the previous chapter, the regular interception of your awareness as it begins to drift away is the foundation of concentration. But it's not a rigid, teeth-gritting, immovable mind focus; rather it's the awareness of your thoughts taking over and reeling your attention back in over and over again that gives the illusion of a hard focus.

As with self-discipline, concentration grows with repeated practice and use. Meditation is, therefore, an ideal training environment to build your ability to focus awareness and concentration. Whenever you draw your attention back to the mantra you strengthen the neural pathways and thicken the brain regions associated with concentration and attention span. With time and practice, concentration is impacted in two significant ways.

1. It can be maintained for longer periods and while being confronted with more distractions.
2. It begins to grow deeper, creating what is known as one-pointed attention. This quality of concentration is spoken of in Chapter 6, Verse 19 of the *Bhagavad Gita* when Krishna says, "When meditation is mastered, the mind is unwavering like the flame of a lamp in a windless place."

Just like a puppy on a leash, the mind can be trained by repeatedly bringing it back to the object of attention. But remember, it's just a light tug on the leash, not a hard yank. Our concentration during meditation is a soft focus. No effort, no strain, no struggle. A light nudge to the mantra is all it takes. With practice, concentration grows and the mind becomes a trusted friend rather than an unruly tenant living in your head.

The third pillar is the combined attributes of *insight, wisdom, and intuition*. *Insight* is the ability to have a penetrating understanding of a situation, relationship, or experience. It's the expansion of awareness to perceive the larger picture and see things with greater clarity and depth. Similarly, *wisdom* implies the application of knowledge, experience, good judgment, discernment, and perceptiveness. Slightly different is *intuition*, which is the ability to have deep understanding of something immediately, free from reasoning or thinking things through. It is more of an instinctive feeling or awareness that arises spontaneously. The development of these related qualities goes hand in hand with the practice of meditation in several ways.

1. By its very nature, meditation is a practice that expands awareness. In the settling down of the thinking process into stillness, we see more deeply into the nature of things and gain a broader perspective. In the same way that we adjust a radio dial to clear up the static or distortions in a radio signal, meditation cleans up the signals we are receiving, both from our external environment as well as our subjective mental space. When our mental turbulence subsides, even briefly, we are able to glimpse a more profound reality that often lies hidden beneath the whirlwind of mental activity.
2. Through the simple and regular act of paying attention, we are able to "sense" more—whether it's in the form of our traditional five senses of hearing, touch, sight, taste, or smell, or the more subtle sense of intuition that helps us tune in to deeper, more

refined sensations that arise from a more instinctual or gut level of awareness. Intuition after all, is simply a heightened sensitivity to signals and impressions registered in the body as urges or knowing that serve as an internal guidance system. Through meditative awareness, we are more able to feel and register those intuitive cues when they arise.

3. As we continue to dip into the gap or the transcendental field of awareness, we are essentially plugging into the cosmic database that is the infinite repository of all that was, is, and ever will be. With regular practice this open channel can facilitate what is sometimes referred to as *spontaneous knowing*, or a sudden perceptive download of insight into a situation, an object, relationship, or the inner workings of your mind and the nature of the world. As the Buddha noted: "Meditation brings wisdom; lack of mediation leaves ignorance. Know well what leads you forward and what holds you back, and choose the path that leads to wisdom."

The fourth pillar of meditation practice is *compassion* and what the Buddhist tradition calls *loving kindness*. The definition of compassion is "to suffer with," meaning having sympathy and feeling the sorrow or pain of another, but also wishing to alleviate the suffering. Compassion has long been associated with the practice of meditation. The motivation of the future Buddha, Prince Sidhartha, to seek expanded states of consciousness and enlightenment was the desire to find an answer and cure to human suffering. We all know suffering as a part of our lives. It is also a natural and healthy human desire to help relieve the suffering of others.

Loving kindness is similar to compassion; however, it embodies more of a tenderness of spirit and abiding consideration for others. It is a feeling of genuine goodwill and affection toward all beings. Often referred to as *metta* in the Buddhist tradition, loving kindness is a quality that resides deep within each of us; however, the stress and tensions of daily life often overshadow its presence.

Meditation practice is correlated to compassion and loving kindness in two important ways.

1. As we regularly tap into the stillness of our soul, we experience the softening of the perceived boundaries between ourselves and the external world. We feel a sense of merging with our surroundings, the environment, and other beings. We begin to sense a deep interconnectedness between all things. There is a sutra in Sanskrit, *Tat Tvam Asi*, which means "I am that, you are that, all this is that, and that's all there is." When you begin to feel the world as your extended body, you become more attuned and sensitive to the pain and suffering of others. You understand that we're all in this together and lessening the suffering of another helps us all.

2. Through meditation you are expressing and deepening your capacity for *self-compassion*. Self-compassion is simply the willingness and ability to give ourselves the care, love, and nourishment that we would for another. Think about it for a moment—how often do we treat ourselves with the kindness or care that we would show a good friend or loved one? Many of us are our own worst critic, judge ourselves too harshly, and don't treat ourselves with the understanding, love, or forgiveness we would another. But through meditation, we give ourselves the compassion and loving kindness that we deserve just as much as anyone else. We have a chance to rest, to connect deeply with our deepest selves, to let go of old pains, and be easy with ourselves. As much as we tend to think of compassion in terms of giving it to others, the truth is, if we are unable to give it to ourselves, we won't be effective at giving it to anyone else.

Meditation is both an act of compassion for self and others as well as a means to deepen it. It reveals the profound understanding that everyone we meet has known joys and sorrows, just like us. They have known triumphs and failures, just like us. They have lost friends and loved ones, just like us. They have experienced sickness and pain, just like us. And one day, they will die, just like us. This is the great teaching of loving kindness and compassion that lies at the heart of meditation.

The qualities of self-discipline, concentration, insight/wisdom/intuition, and compassion and loving kindness make up the core attributes of a meditation practice. They enhance our meditation and are simultaneously strengthened by it. With this knowledge in tow, let's proceed and answer the question, "What's in it for me?" by exploring the numerous and exciting benefits of a regular meditation practice.

PART 2
WHAT ARE THE BENEFITS?

CHAPTER 4

THE PHYSICAL BENEFITS OF MEDITATION

Now that we've explored how to meditate, the experiences you can expect, and its core attributes, let's take an in-depth look at the benefits to practicing meditation. These benefits come in three general categories: 1) physical, 2) mental and emotional, and 3) spiritual. We'll dedicate a chapter to each of these categories so that you can really grasp the powerful reasons that meditation is such a valuable approach to integrated well-being. We'll begin by delving into the physical benefits.

But before we look at the specific benefits, let me ask you a question. If you had to describe the reason most people in our modern world would want to learn to meditate in one word, what would it be? If you answered S-T-R-E-S-S, you'd be correct. Of course not everyone chooses to learn meditation to cope with stress, but it's a leading motivator for the majority of the meditating public.

We've all experienced stress and have our own unique and intimate relationship with it. Stress takes different forms for different people, but the feeling of, and our reaction to, stress is the same for all of us. But just what is stress? Despite the fact that we all have firsthand experiences of it, sometimes on a daily basis, we often have difficulty describing exactly what stress is. Let's take a moment to understand and explore the meaning of the term to arrive at a definition we can refer back to throughout the next few chapters.

To start with a somewhat simplistic and tongue-in-cheek definition, stress might be described as, "The confusion created when one's mind overrides the body's basic desire to choke the living daylights out of somebody who desperately needs it." Although not a technical definition, we can all probably identify with a time during which we wanted to unleash our own personal hell on someone or something that was obstructing or standing in the way of us fulfilling our needs. However, in our society, we have learned to restrain physical and emotional outbursts that aren't considered appropriate. This feeling of wanting to explode without an outlet is a hallmark of the stress response that this image suggests.

From a more literal perspective, the term stress was coined by Hans Selye, MD, a pioneering endocrinologist who was looking for a way to describe the "state of mental and emotional strain or tension resulting from adverse or very demanding circumstances." The word was originally used in metallurgy to describe the pressure or force put upon a piece of metal as it was being bent out of shape—an appropriate metaphor for what stress does to us.

Selye noted that there are actually two types of stress.

1. The first is what's considered "good" stress or *eustress* and refers to the excitement or thrill that comes from doing something beneficial or fulfilling. For example, some people thrive under tight deadlines or anticipate the thrill of a roller coaster ride resulting in this type of stress.
2. The second type of stress is the less pleasant type, known as *distress*, or the emotional, mental, and physical overload that arises in a highly challenging situation.

Stress embodies the feeling of an inescapable psychological, emotional, or physical pressure. Think for a moment of a garden hose attached to an outdoor spigot. When we turn on the faucet, water effortlessly flows through the hose to water our lawn, wash a car, or fill a swimming pool. The current of energy (water) is able to go wherever we direct it. Now, imagine before turning on the water you tie a knot in the hose. What happens when the water begins to flow? Naturally, the water is blocked, the pressure begins to build, and sooner or later some part of the system (whether it's the hose springing a leak, the fittings or faucet giving out, or the water pump failing) will break down. This is important to understand because when you think about it, our bodies are essentially big tubes through which energy flows. Biochemical energy flows through our veins, arteries, organs, and digestive systems. Emotional energy flows through more subtle vehicles of moods and feelings. And mental energy moves in the form of thoughts, ideas, memories, desires, and perceptions. When one or more of these channels becomes obstructed, the pressure and strain negatively affects the entire system and eventually causes it to break down.

Another key element to the understanding of stress is its subjective nature. What's stressful for one person may not be for another. For example, perhaps you can remember a time when you were out with a friend in public and you bumped into your boss, your ex, or someone you really didn't like. This encounter might trigger an experience of stress for you. Your friend, however, might be completely unaffected. That's because, at its core, stress is an internal process and always begins with a perception, and is based upon a subjective interpretation rather than an actual external reality. Stress doesn't exist independently of you—it's not as if you are driving to work one morning, having a great day, sailing along, everything's terrific, and suddenly you drive through a cloud of stress and "POW," you freak out. Stress requires our participation in an outside event to *perceive* it as a threat and react to it as such.

David Simon, MD, co-founder of the Chopra Center for Wellbeing used to say that "reality is a selective act of attention and interpretation." What this means is that we are all living in different worlds built entirely upon what we look at (attention) and how we think about it (interpretation). One person sees a rainy day and gets upset because they just washed their car while another gets excited because his lawn needed the water—attention and interpretation. When it comes to stress the perception of a threat is typically activated by the crossing of what we call the *mine*field, or the physical or emotional crossing of our boundary of safety. For many of us that boundary exists physically anywhere from three to five feet from our body and serves as the edge of our ideal personal space. Whenever something breaches that boundary, whether it's physically, mentally, or emotionally, and pushes something unwelcomed into our minefield, it often triggers the perception of a threat. We feel violated, as if something unwanted is being forced upon us. Likewise, whenever something we felt was ours—such as a possession, a relationship, or a title—is removed we feel equally threatened. Thus, the minefield serves as borderland between the perception of safety and danger.

In the final analysis, stress boils down to *the perception of a threat (real or imagined) triggered by our needs not being met*. We are all trying to fulfill our desires, we all have things we need to do or accomplish. But sometimes there is an obstacle that prevents us from getting there. As human beings, our problem-solving nature is such that we want to find or make a way around the obstacle, but if we aren't able to see an alternate means to get there, we feel stuck, frustrated, overwhelmed. Ultimately, this blockage is translated and interpreted by our mind and body as a threat to our very survival, resulting in the stress response we know so well.

CHARACTERISTICS OF THE STRESS RESPONSE

Armed with this definition of stress described above, let's take a look at some of the unique qualities of the stress response and its fundamental purpose.

First, whether we're talking about "good" stress or "bad" stress, both types can be expressed in our lives in a manner that is either acute or chronic. *Acute stress* is the sudden onset of an emergency or threatening situation. Imagine abruptly getting cut off in highway traffic or being mugged at gunpoint. These situations cause an immediate activation of the stress response without any prolonged or anticipated buildup. They happen in seconds with little to no warning. *Chronic stress*, on the other hand, builds up over time and is experienced for a prolonged period. It may take the form of an intense work project or an ongoing relationship challenge that saps the strength and energy of those involved. It's as if you are Atlas, carrying the world on your shoulders, and it gets a little heavier each day.

Second, real stress and imagined stress affect you in a similar way. Obviously, a real-time stressor will have a powerful impact on your mind and body. But stressful situations from the past recalled vividly enough, perhaps during the re-telling to a friend or during an attempt to vent the emotional turbulence experienced, can trigger a repeat of the stressful sensations originally experienced in your physiology. If you doubt this is true, simply close your eyes and in your mind's eye play back with as much detail as possible an argument or confrontation you have had with someone in the past. With little effort, your memories will automatically begin to activate the same physical, mental, and emotional responses that you experienced when the event originally occurred, whether it took place five days or five years ago.

Next, the perception of stress activates what is known as the *fight-or-flight response*. This well-known term was coined by the eminent physiologist Walter Cannon in 1915 to describe the changes that take place in an animal's physiology due to a perceived attack, harmful event, or other threat to its survival. The fight-or-flight response is a state of hyperarousal prompted by the activation of the sympathetic nervous system that prepares the body to either fight or run away. The fight-or-flight response is part of our biological inheritance from our ancient ancestors. When primitive humans were hunting and gathering in the prehistoric past, the fight-or-flight response developed as a primary survival mechanism to ensure that the species would endure. This response allowed our ancestors to either defend themselves or escape to safety in times of danger. If while gathering food you were confronted by a wild animal or an enemy tribesman, the fight-or-flight response gave your body the ability to perform at a higher level in order to survive. Those of our ancestors who were able to activate the fight-or-flight response to ensure their survival passed this mechanism down to future generations, to the present day.

Due to its association to stress, the fight-or-flight response often gets a bad rap. However, despite no longer living in a prehistoric era, we still need and rely on this function of our nervous system. If you've ever heard superhuman stories of a mother lifting a car off her child or someone rushing into a burning building to rescue a puppy, these people were tapping into the physiological changes brought about through the fight-or-flight response. Similarly, if you serve in the military, law enforcement, or some branch of fire rescue or EMT services, you don't want to be without the fight-or-flight response as it may save your life. Indeed, such individuals must not only rely on this response, but also learn how to manage it for optimum performance in the field.

So the fight-or-flight response is ultimately a good thing. Unfortunately, we can run into problems when we either activate this response too often or neglect to turn it off. It was meant to be a contingency plan for our physiology, not the primary operating system. Fight-or-flight functioning evolved to be switched on to save the day and then turned back off once the danger had passed. What's more, the effects of this response were largely burned out of our ancestors' system during the act of fighting or fleeing. Once the crisis had been averted they could return to hunting and gathering or painting cave walls. Fast forward to the present day—not only can we activate the fight-or-flight response between five to fifteen times a day, but we do so *not because our lives are being threatened* (although this might happen), but rather due to a frustrating or overwhelming life event that *we interpret* as life threatening. For example, dealing with a traffic jam on the drive to work, too many voice messages or emails, a rude cashier at the store, a sudden project or deadline thrown into your lap at the last minute, a snarky comment to your post on a social media site, or a disagreement with a neighbor or spouse can all elicit the perception of stress and the consequential activation of the fight-or-flight response. In none of these situations is our actual physical well-being in danger, however, through years of practice, we have created a conditioned interpretation that sends the signal to your physiology to "Go to war!" What's more, without the stress-balancing effect of running, fighting, or other intense physical activity, the effects of the fight-or-flight response lingers in our system for hours, perhaps even days, before dissipating and returning the mind-body system to a state of non-stressed equilibrium.

Fortunately, most of the examples above fall into the acute stress category, which means that once the stress is over the body and mind will eventually return to a more balanced state. However, when chronic stress is involved, the fight-or-flight response never truly powers down long enough to give the body a chance to reset. In such cases this seemingly endless hypervigilant state becomes an all-too-familiar experience for many people in our fast-paced world.

I've heard it said that if you place a frog in a pot of boiling water, it will immediately jump out because it instantly recognizes the danger it's in. However, if you place a frog in cold water and slowly raise the temperature to boiling, the frog will allow itself to be cooked to death because the change is too gradual to perceive until it's too late. Now, I don't know whether this is factually accurate or not, but the point is still clear. If we had arrived into this world having experienced little to no stress, we would likely immediately recoil at the levels of stress in our daily lives. Having progressively increased the levels of stress we are subjected to on a regular basis, we have sadly become more numb to the warning signs of these consistently higher levels of stress.

The result is that through practice and acquiescence we have come to accept this situation as "normal." We tell ourselves that we live in a stressful world and it's "just the way things are." When asked how we're doing, we automatically reply with "Oh, it's another stressful day at the office" as if it was of little or no concern. But it *is* of concern, and as you'll discover in the next section it can quite literally become a life-or-death matter.

THE PHYSIOLOGY OF THE FIGHT-OR-FLIGHT RESPONSE (THE BAD NEWS)

It's important to understand that the activation of the fight-or-flight response represents a complete 180-degree change in our biological operating system. It causes a total reorganization of multiple physiological systems to prioritize survival over all other concerns. Following the initial perception of a threat this switch-up in function is initiated by what's often described as a *chemical cascade* in which key hormones and neurological messenger molecules sound the alarm through the entire body. Within a few heartbeats, your whole mind-body system is gearing up for danger.

What follows is a rough breakdown of what takes place in your body as you prepare for a life-threatening encounter. This is not an exhaustive list as so many fundamental changes are taking place that an overly detailed explanation is beyond the scope of this book. Also, while I've listed these physiological events in somewhat of a sequential order, understand that these changes are all happening virtually instantaneously over the span of just a few seconds.

- **Perception of a threat:** A message is received through the senses (or recalled in memory) that is interpreted as dangerous and threatening.

- **Stress hormones are released:** Messenger molecules signal the release of two heavy-hitter chemicals: adrenaline and cortisol. Secreted from the brain and the adrenal glands, these chemicals are the triggers to prime your body for immediate physical action by boosting strength, enhancing responsiveness, and surging energy levels. You can think of these chemicals as the rocket fuel of your body. They are meant to deliver a powerful punch and burn intensely through the system for a short period of time.
- **Increased respiration:** As we prepare to exert ourselves in fight-or-flight mode, our respiration level increases dramatically. Breathing becomes quick and short to boost the volume of oxygen getting into the system.
- **Increased heart rate:** To move the increased levels of oxygen, stress hormones, and glucose throughout the body, the heart begins to pump faster and harder.
- **Increased blood pressure:** The increased pulmonary and cardiac demand constricts circulatory vessels, raising blood pressure levels.
- **Sweating/perspiration:** Elevated heartbeat and respiration levels increase body heat and trigger a sweating response to keep the body cool.
- **Increased platelet stickiness:** These small blood cells are responsible for binding together when we get cut to form a blood clot and to stop bleeding. During the fight-or-flight response, the blood cells increase their stickiness in preparation for injury, making the blood thicker and more viscous.
- **Redirected blood flow:** During non–life-threatening situations, a large portion of our blood supply circulates in and around our torso, supporting the major organs and the high energy demands of the digestive process. When we activate the fight-or-flight response, the blood supply is directed *away* from the digestive organs and into the arms and legs in preparation for running or

fighting. This sudden reallocation of circulation has a directly noticeable manifestation—the familiar clenching of your abdominal muscles followed by the sensation of your stomach leaping into your throat. The digestive system grinds to a hard stop, suspending the metabolism of your last meal until the perceived danger has passed.

- **Increased muscular tension:** In preparation for fighting or fleeing, our large skeletal muscles prime themselves for action with an elevated level of tightness. Like a Western gunfighter's hand twitching before hearing the word "Draw!" our muscles maintain a heightened level of rigidity in anticipation of explosive and violent movement.
- **Increased blood sugar and fat are released into the system:** Triggered by the stress hormones, the liver dumps sugar and fat stores into the bloodstream to be burned as fuel for the body's higher physical demands. This process cuts down on insulin production and prevents glucose from being stored in favor of being utilized immediately by the body. As a related byproduct, those same hormones signal the digestive system to consume additional sugar and fat as reserve fuel. While in fight-or-flight mode the body essentially doesn't know when or where its next meal will come from and therefore craves the consumption of "instant energy" foods (aka carbohydrates and fats) to maintain its higher level of performance until the crisis subsides.
- **Suppressed immunity:** The immune system consumes an enormous amount of energy fighting off environmental toxins, pollutants, and opportunistic bacteria and viruses. During prolonged fight-or-flight operations, however, that energy is required elsewhere in the body and the immune function is weakened. (Immunity does increase briefly while under acute stress however, chronic stress leads to profoundly compromised immune function.) The immediate threat concern is staying alive to get

home safely; therefore, fighting off a cold, virus, or the flu is not a priority.
- **Accelerated aging:** The stress response and its hormones take a high toll on the overall function and longevity of the body. Prolonged stress can damage cells, lead to premature hearing and vision loss, and contribute to the breakdown of DNA. If you have any doubt this is true, simply compare photographs taken at the beginning and ending of a president's term of office to witness the marked age accelerating effects of stress on the body.
- **Repressed sex drive:** The elevated levels of cortisol in the body can suppress the body's natural sex hormones. In much the same way the fight-or-flight response powers down the immune system, it also shuts off the libido and any urge to reproduce. As long as the perception of threat dominates, sex isn't a priority.
- **The body operates in protection mode:** Figuratively speaking, we can generally think of the body operating in either a growth or protection mode at any given time. Growth mode is a state in which the body is able to rest, digest, repair itself, and maintain a state of wholeness and balance. Protection mode, on the other hand, is a defensive physical and mental posture marked by hypersensitivity, tension, anxiety, and the aforementioned fight-or-flight characteristics. Our bodies can only operate in one mode at a time and, while under stress, protection mode is the only option.
- **Perpetual threat perception:** Over time, the fight-or-flight response becomes habitually programed into our body and nervous system as the go-to operating mode whenever we are confronted with stress. Like any conditioned behavior, the more often we activate it, the more normal it becomes until we are "tuned" to continually perceive the world as a threatening place. Constantly on the lookout for the next danger, we filter the entire world through a slightly paranoid, on-guard, and defensive lens.

Again, while there are additional stress factors that could be added to this list, it paints a general picture of the myriad changes that take place in our bodies when we're under the fight-or-flight response. The sum total of these changes is what Dr. David Simon called *sowing the seeds of illness*, a term meant to point out the causative or correlative relationship between the prolonged activation of the fight-or-flight response and decreased health. When we look closely at any of the physiological changes described previously it quickly becomes apparent how they relate to the major diseases affecting our society today:

Physiological Change	May Cause or Contribute To
Increased stress hormones	Anxiety, depression, memory and cognitive impairment, insomnia, muscle tension, premature aging
Increased heart rate, elevated blood pressure	Coronary heart disease, stroke, inflammatory response
Stickier platelets	Blood clots, heart attacks, stroke
Redirected digestive circulation	Digestive problems: IBS, heartburn
Increased blood sugar/fat	Diabetes, obesity, inflammatory response, difficulty losing weight
Suppressed immunity	Colds, viruses, infections, allergies, cancer
Perpetual threat perception	Anxiety, PTSD, chronic fatigue

It's probably apparent now why I referred to this section as "the bad news." Most of us all have some levels of stress in our lives and we instinctively know that stress is bad for us. But reading this list often causes us to become even more stressed knowing just what it's doing to us. Rest assured that's not my intention. However, I feel this knowledge is invaluable when it comes to our overall health and well-being. If you get nothing else from this chapter beyond the understanding of just how deadly stress is to our bodies over the long run, I'll be happy.

THE PHYSICAL BENEFITS OF MEDITATION 73

Regardless, don't let yourself get too overwhelmed by the effects stress may be having on your life. After all, you've already learned to meditate and that in and of itself has a dramatic effect on the way stress affects your body. Let's take a look at that now.

THE PHYSIOLOGY OF MEDITATION (THE GOOD NEWS)

Having established that stress and the resulting changes in our body due to the fight-or-flight response are poisonous to our overall health and well-being, we can breathe a sigh of relief knowing that meditation is quite literally the antidote to stress. For all intents and purposes, the practice of meditation reverses nearly all of the physiological changes mentioned in the previous section. Activation of the restful awareness response ushers in the complete opposite effect of stress on our body. While stress signals our body to fight or run, meditation signals our body to rest and digest.

Let's take a second look at the systems affected by the fight-or-flight response and see how radically different they operate during the restful awareness state. As with the previous list, these details will provide a fundamental understanding of the physical benefits of meditation. But as research on meditation is ever deepening our understanding, there will undoubtedly be more insights gained in the years to come.

During meditation our physical body experiences the following:

- **Slowed and soothed respiration:** As our mind and body relax, our breathing becomes slower and deeper, reflecting the mind's less turbulent state. At times it may even feel as if the breath stops. This is due in part to a marked decrease in the body's need for oxygen, dropping 10 percent to 25 percent lower than normal during meditation. This reduced oxygen consumption also contributes to a lower metabolic rate known as *hypo-metabolism*. This state can create a deeper and more profound experience of bodily rest than sleep, leading many meditators to feel more rested following twenty minutes of meditation than after twenty minutes of sleep.

- **Lowered heart rate:** As the body relaxes, the output of the heart, compared to when it is experiencing the fight-or-flight response, is significantly lower. Lower levels of mental and physical exertion put less strain on the heart and allow it to beat at a more moderate pace. There is also evidence that meditation improves *heart rate variability* (HRV). HRV is the naturally occurring irregularity of the heart rate. Higher levels of HRV are indicative of lower stress levels, higher resiliency, and overall good heart health. Lower HRV is associated with higher levels of stress and overall cardiovascular risk. Research indicates that meditation may have a beneficial effect on this important marker of heart health.
- **Lowered blood pressure:** Hypertension or high blood pressure (also known as the silent killer) is at epidemic proportions in our society. Fortunately, regular meditation can have a noticeable effect on lowering blood pressure. One of the key contributing factors to high blood pressure is stress, and as the stress response is mitigated through meditation, blood pressure naturally lowers as well. As noted in Herbert Benson, MD's *The Relaxation Response*, studies indicate that patients who suffered from hypertension saw a decrease in blood pressure through the regular practice of meditation. Note: I am not recommending that if you have high blood pressure, you stop taking your medication. Always seek the guidance of your health care provider when dealing with your personal treatment options. However, I can tell you that I have known meditators, some of whom are my students, who have noted a decrease in their blood pressure after a period of regular meditation practice, an improvement that was also applauded by their physicians.

- **Reduced perspiration and sweating:** Since the body is no longer going into survival overdrive, its temperature is more regulated and balanced and the clammy stress sweat is no longer required to dissipate the body's excess heat. In fact, during meditation the body may even become slightly cool or chilly due to the decreased physical activity and lowered oxygen consumption.
- **Stress chemicals eliminated:** During the fight-or-flight response, stress hormones such as cortisol and adrenaline are maintained at a high level for as long as the stress persists. In the case of chronic stress, those elevated levels may last for days or even weeks before slowly being flushed out of the system. The restful awareness response (brought on through meditation) triggers the stress release mechanisms and sends the signal of peace and tranquility to every cell in the body, thereby notifying the endocrine system to stand down from red alert and eliminate the excess stress hormones naturally and effortlessly.
- **Platelets become less sticky:** As we've seen, during periods of stress, platelet activation increases to prepare for the possibility of injury or physical trauma. However, once meditation and the restful awareness response begins to reorder the body's processes to a more calm and balanced state, the platelets "loosen up" and become less prone to clump or form potentially dangerous artery-obstructing clots. This reduces the blood's viscosity or internal friction, allowing it to flow more easily and reduce the amount of effort required by the heart.
- **Circulation returns to a more balanced and healthy function:** With the signals of danger turned off, the circulatory system directs the blood flow away from the arms and legs and back to the internal organs for digestion, metabolism, regulation, and physical restoration. Muscular tension is reduced and the arms and legs are able to relax deeply. This relaxation can be especially profound,

and upon completing meditation you may notice the distinct lack of feeling in the extremities until they become active once again.
- **Blood sugar and fat return to lower and more balanced levels:** As stress is mitigated, the need for excess fuel in the bloodstream is lowered, reducing the demand on the liver and restoring healthy insulin levels. The desire for sweets and fats is lessened and food intake becomes more normalized.
- **Strengthened immune function:** The practice of meditation not only helps to restore healthy immune function by counteracting the effects of stress, but also helps to improve overall immunity above baseline levels. Meditation has been shown to boost disease-fighting antibodies as well as stimulate parts of the brain associated with overall immune function, helping the immune system to operate more effectively.
- **Decreased inflammation:** In recent years, science has come to recognize the damaging effect chronic inflammation has on our overall health and well-being. Prolonged activation of the body's inflammatory response (closely tied to the fight-or-flight response) is directly related to a host of chronic conditions such as cardiovascular disease, metabolic syndrome, obesity, type 2 diabetes, Alzheimer's disease, autoimmune disorders, and some cancers. Fortunately, recent studies have found that meditation practice reduces the expression (or turns off) genes related to inflammation and stress-related genetic pathways. Through meditation we simultaneously reduce our stress levels and suppress the inflammatory response down to the cellular level!
- **Slowed and reversed aging:** By balancing the endocrine system and reducing the levels of stress hormones in our bodies, meditation helps to reverse the stress-related damage caused by overexposure to the fight-or-flight response. But the good news doesn't stop there. Research conducted by the Transcendental Meditation (TM) Organization has demonstrated that meditators who had

been practicing consistently for five years or more were *twelve years younger* physiologically than their biological peers. The mechanism by which this happen may be revealed through the study of *telomeres*, the end caps of our chromosomes. Like the plastic tips at the end of a shoelace, telomeres help protect our DNA from wear and tear. Stress can cause a great deal of damage to our telomeres. However, it appears that meditation may help to increase telomerase (the enzyme that repairs and strengthens telomeres). This means that regular meditation may help to keep our telomeres healthy, thereby prolonging the life of our DNA, our cells, and our bodies.

- **Restored sex drive:** Through the experience of restful awareness, the body's danger network is downgraded allowing the sex drive to return to normal. Additionally, levels of key sex-boosting hormones such as dehydroepiandrosterone (DHEA), human growth hormone (HGH), and testosterone are enhanced through the practice of meditation.
- **Body operates in growth mode:** De-escalating the stress response through meditation allows the body to switch from protection mode into growth mode. Homeostatic balance is restored and the body naturally begins to repair, rest, and nourish the entire physiology. This is the rest-and-digest mode of functioning that is key to overall health and well-being.
- **Increased energy:** Due to the all-hands-on-deck, spastic nature of the fight-or-flight response, our bodies use energy in an inefficient manner. This increased physiological demand is what requires the release of additional blood sugar and fat discussed earlier. Perhaps you can remember a time when you were mentally or emotionally stressed and at the end of that period, you may have collapsed out of sheer exhaustion even though the situation wasn't actually physically demanding. This is because the fight-or-flight network sucked your physiological energy system dry as it was poised for

a life-or-death struggle. However, when the stress response is mitigated through meditation, our bodies return to homeostatic balance that regulates the most efficient use of energy for balance and optimal function.
- **Minimized threat perception:** The on-guard mind and body state brought about by stress is powered down during meditation. Through regular practice, our tendency to interpret the world as perpetually dangerous and threatening is reduced, and we are able to experience life in a more calm, peaceful, and secure manner.

All told, I think you can see this is an impressive list of beneficial physiological changes that are brought about through the practice of meditation. Put together, these benefits activate what we could refer to as the *inner pharmacy*, or the body's natural and inborn resource to heal and restore itself to an optimum and balanced function. The potential for health, strength, vitality, and longevity is already within each of us. The trick is tapping into the body's wisdom to release that potential. By reducing stress and activating the restful awareness response meditation is a powerful means to trigger the healer within. While I'm not suggesting that meditation is a cure-all or that you should ignore your doctor's recommendations and try to meditate away a serious or life-threatening illness, I do believe that meditation can provide tangible physical benefits for anyone who makes it a regular part of their life and I eagerly look forward to the day when the benefits listed above are recognized by the medical establishment as a worthy complement to traditional forms of treatment.

If you chose to practice meditation solely for the benefits described above, it would undoubtedly be a worthwhile investment of your time and energy. However, if you're not yet convinced, and your only takeaway from this chapter has been the deadly impact of unmanaged stress on our lives and the need to do something about it, I'll be satisfied. But if you want to dig deeper into the benefits meditation can bring to our lives, stick with me—and let's continue our exploration in the next chapter.

> *If meditation were a drug, it would be considered medical malpractice to fail to prescribe it.*
> —Dawson Church, PhD

CHAPTER 5

THE MENTAL AND EMOTIONAL BENEFITS OF MEDITATION

As we start to probe deeper into the effects of meditation on our minds and emotions, it's helpful to recognize that these layers exist in a slightly more subtle realm of our lives. Thoughts, emotions, moods, perceptions, and states of awareness are not on the gross level of our physical bodies and can take on a more subjective and experiential quality than the hard and solid aspects of our bodies we examined in the previous chapter. They are, however, no less important or relevant to our understanding of meditation's benefits.

But before we discuss the benefits themselves, let's take few moments to look at where we presently find ourselves when it comes to using our minds, emotions, and awareness on a day-to-day basis. This is what I refer to as our *current state of inattention*. We in our modern society know this place well and are intimately familiar with its effects, if even only on a subconscious level. Here's a quick summary of what we're putting our attention on nearly every day of our lives:

- Daily routine: Starting our day, following a morning ritual, exercise, seeing to meals, travel, general tasks and chores
- Family/relationships: Husbands, wives, boyfriends or girlfriends, children, parents, close friends, pets, neighbors and acquaintances

- Career/job: Responsibilities, organizing, managing, guiding/leading others, working, emails, phone calls/voicemails, meetings, deadlines
- Daily commute: Driving/carpooling, public transit, traffic, distracted driving, angry drivers
- Online presence: Email, texts, web browsing, social media
- Entertainment/personal time: Television, movies, music, video games, socializing
- Unexpected issues: Minor crises, stresses, anxiety, disturbances, full-blown emergencies

All of these things and potentially more contribute to an increasingly overwhelmed mental state that many of us experience on a regular basis. We are bombarded with an enormous amount of information each and every day, far more than any time in human history. Our parents, grandparents, or great-grandparents lived lives far removed from the tidal wave of raw data that we are exposed to in our daily lives. That's not to say they didn't experience stress—they did; however, it's safe to say they didn't have to mentally process as much or as quickly as we do in the modern information age.

But saying we've got a lot going on in our lives doesn't do this situation justice. Let's dig a little deeper.

For example, consider just how much information we're receiving through our five senses alone at any given time. It's been estimated that we're exposed to roughly 400 billion bits of information per second, and about 2,000 of those bits make it through to the level of our conscious awareness. Those bits make up all the sensations we register in our nervous system such as the temperature of the air on our skin, the amount of light entering our eyes, the background noises in the environment, the pressure of our body in a chair, the odors detected by our nose, or tastes on our tongue. This is an astonishing amount of information coming at us in every moment, just on the sensory level.

THE MENTAL AND EMOTIONAL BENEFITS OF MEDITATION

Amazingly, our brain is able to sort through all those bits and determine if they are important enough to consciously register or remain washed out in the background. And add to the mix the frequency of distractions we encounter at any given time. With all these nearly simultaneous signals being processed by our nervous system, the fact that we're able to get anything accomplished seems nothing short of miraculous.

To add another layer to this quagmire, think back to those 60,000 to 80,000 thoughts we have every day. Not only do those thoughts keep coming in an uninterrupted stream like BBs being bounced off your forehead, many of those thoughts are either 1) the same thoughts you had yesterday or 2) negative or self-destructive in nature. What this means is that a great deal of our precious daily attention reserves are being consumed by a repetitive playback of previous thoughts or thoughts that are haunting or hurting us. Talk about adding insult to injury.

Before you get too depressed, however, it may be helpful to know that while many of our thoughts can be negative, it not necessarily our fault, so to speak. This is because we have what it known as a *negativity bias*. Our brains are more sensitive to negative events and thoughts than they are to positive ones. Believe it or not, the brain is drawn to bad news rather good. As a byproduct of the survival mechanism inherently built into our biology, our brains evolved to be more alert to situations that were negative so we could avoid danger. It's not likely that our ancient ancestors were able to sit around a campfire and enjoy a nice meal with friends under a beautiful starry sky the way that we do today because they had to be on the lookout for any threats to their survival. The fire, food, friends, or stars might distract them from the threat of a wild animal or an attack by an enemy tribe.

Unfortunately, we have unwittingly inherited this predisposition toward the negative and can easily come under its sway if we're not careful. It's easy to be negative; it takes effort to override this tendency and look for the positive in and around our lives.

To add to our current state of inattention is the disheartening fact that human beings seem to have an ever-increasing aversion to doing one thing at a time. When I was twelve years old, my favorite TV show was *Buck Rogers in the 25th Century*. I vividly remember sprawling out on our living room floor with my brother, our chins resting in our hands, eyes glued to the television, eager to see what adventure Gil Gerard and Erin Gray would find themselves in each exciting episode. For us there was nothing else happening in the world. Buck Rogers was our world in that moment.

Things have changed. Now, while most of us watch our favorite programs, what are we doing? We're likely eating a meal, texting, playing a video game, talking on the phone, or scrolling through our feed on social media. We don't simply watch our favorite shows anymore. In our modern information society, we've become allergic to doing just one thing at a time. And this doesn't apply only to television. In fact, most of our daily goings-on are forced to compete with numerous other things being performed simultaneously. Whether we're eating a meal, driving our cars, fulfilling our daily work responsibilities, or spending time with our friends and family, we often find ourselves dividing our attention between two or three other activities. There's a word for doing several things at once like this—multitasking—and it's doing far more harm than good.

Most of us are familiar with multitasking. We may even pride ourselves on our ability to juggle several competing tasks at once. And why shouldn't we? The business and professional worlds have come to treat multitasking as a highly valuable skill set. For example, when looking to fill a job opening, many employers will tell you they are seeking someone with a "demonstrated ability to handle multiple tasks in a fast-paced environment." But here's the catch—our conscious minds can't do it! That's right, *multitasking is an illusion*. The conscious mind

THE MENTAL AND EMOTIONAL BENEFITS OF MEDITATION

that thinks rational thoughts, makes decisions, and understands information is a *serial processor*, meaning it attends to and processes one item at a time. The more you give your conscious mind to do at any given moment, the weaker and less effective it becomes.

I can hear the protests from the high-performance achievers who claim with certainty that they are capable of multitasking and even excel at it. What they believe, however, is the simultaneous performance of several things at once is actually their brain's ability to quickly shift from one focus of attention to another. While this quick shifting of attention can give one the illusion of multitasking, it doesn't change the fact that it's not the most optimum and efficient use of our brains. Doing one thing at a time with our full attention is a far more effective way to perform any activity. Increasing the task load on the conscious mind in this way only contributes to our state of inattention.

Let's take a quick look at some interesting multitasking statistics:[1]

- Studies show that only 2 percent of people can actually multitask effectively.
- Eighty-nine percent of people with smartphones use them at work, even though 45 percent of US workers believe they have to work on too many things at once.
- On average, employees who use a computer for work are distracted once every 10.5 minutes.
- Sixty-two percent of web pages students open on their laptops during class are unrelated to the subject.
- On average, students generate sixty-five new screen windows per lecture.
- While average Americans watch TV, they're also doing other tasks: 42 percent browse the internet, 29 percent talk on the phone, and 26 percent text or IM.

- When it comes to checking email or the internet via smartphone, 67 percent will do so on a date, 45 percent will at the movie theater, and 33 percent will in church.
- Trying to focus on more than one thing at once causes a 40 percent drop in productivity.
- Studies show that while working, being distracted by incoming calls or emails lowers a person's IQ by ten points (the equivalent to missing a night of sleep and twice the effect of smoking marijuana).
- The average desk job employee loses 2.1 hours a day to interruptions or distractions, adding up to a total of 546 hours lost annually.
- Students who do homework while IMing or texting are more likely to report academic impairment.
- Using a cell phone (handheld or handsfree) delays a driver's reaction time by as much as having a blood alcohol content of .08 percent.
- Multitasking confuses your brain and slows things down: concentrating on one task at a time will get the job done much faster.

Multitasking is not the way to go if you want to perform at your brain's most efficient level. Further, despite our ability to constantly learn new things multitasking is not a skill that gets better over time. As Deepak Chopra puts it, "Multitasking is the only thing that gets worse with practice."

Consider one last thing regarding our current state of inattention: our brain/mind system is an extraordinary organ capable of incredible feats of processing and information management. But like a computer, it has a maximum operating speed that cannot be exceeded without consequences. Think for a moment about what happens when you're in a rush and you turn on your computer and try to open several programs or apps at once. Even the fastest computers have an operating threshold that, when exceeded, will freeze or fail, informing the user that the requested program is unable to respond. It's unable to respond because we've pushed the computer past its functional limits. And although the human brain far outclasses even the most sophisticated computers, there's absolutely no reason to believe it behaves any differently when it's forced to process more information than it's designed to handle.

In a nutshell, our current mental state is overloaded, biased toward the negative, rife with distractions, and multitasked to the hilt. If we distill all these causes down to a resulting effect what do we have? As with the previous chapter, let's look at some of the mental and emotional imbalances this environment contributes to.

- **A distinct loss of focus and mental clarity:** As a byproduct of consistent information overload, we often feel as if we are in a fog; our awareness is unfocused, blurry, and lacking the ability to perceive the world and ourselves distinctly and lucidly.
- **Hazy/washed-out awareness:** Like a beam of light, our awareness can be weak and dim on one hand or bright, powerful, and tightly focused on the other. Think of the light shining from a floodlight or perhaps an old, barely functioning florescent tube. It would be murky, dim, and perhaps a little gloomy. In that light you might feel heavy, unmotivated, or maybe even depressed. In a similar way, when watered down or fragmented, as our awareness often is, we see only a partial and somewhat melancholic quality of the world. It's like looking through a dirty window – our view will always be somewhat obscured by our lowered quality of awareness.
- **Inability to pay attention:** In our overloaded mental environment our ability to concentrate on one thing at a time is severely compromised. We struggle to pay attention, are distracted by the smallest interruption, and feel as if a mental hurricane is whirling through our minds 24/7. This state has given way to an epidemic of ADD and ADHD in our society. These disorders, by definition mean that one has consistently low levels of *attention*.

It seems odd when you think about it, that you could run out of attention as if it were gas in your car or some other type of fuel. But attention is like your mind's fuel. It is a precious commodity that we need to conserve and use carefully. As entrepreneur and expert in data-driven innovation Alistair Croll astutely observes, "An environment with excess information devours the one thing that information truly demands: attention." When we continually bombard our minds with too much data, these "diseases of distraction" become rampant.

- **Poor decision-making:** Too much information obscures our ability to tap into our higher brain functions and make good, clear choices. With our minds barely treading water in a deluge of potential options, it becomes all too easy to get caught up in analysis paralysis on one end of the spectrum or impulsive and rash decision-making on the other. Either way, our mental processing is severely dampened and the choices we make will often be less than ideal.

- **Susceptibility to emotional hijacking, reactivity, and control dramas:** With less clear thinking comes a diminished control over our emotional state. The brain's limbic system is what governs our emotional lives and our higher mental functions. But when the main processor is overloaded, the limbic system is more vulnerable to old emotional habits and reactive behaviors. These reactive emotional habits are known as *control dramas* and consist of manipulative strategies that we fall into when our needs aren't being met. Control dramas are frequently learned in childhood as a means to get others to give you what you want. There are four primary types of control dramas:

    1. Being nice and manipulative
    2. Being nasty and manipulative
    3. Being aloof and withdrawn
    4. Playing the victim or poor-me role

Let me give you an example of how this works. Imagine that you are a small child at a theme park. You and your parents have had an exciting day and now you're heading home. On the way out of the park, you notice a giant spiral lollipop as big as your head. You immediately decide you must have it, so you petition your parents to get it for you. Your mother/father says, "No, you can't have the lollipop, you've had enough sugar today and you'll spoil your dinner."

You then try the first control drama and reply, "But mommy/daddy, if you get it for me, I promise to be good, and go to bed on time, and to be nice to my brother" (nice and manipulative).

Your parents hold their ground and refuse to give in.

You change tactics to the second control drama and promptly throw a temper tantrum, crying, screaming, stomping around, and making a scene (nasty and manipulative).

Scolding you for your outburst, your parents still aren't giving in to get the lollipop. With the failure of the first two strategies, you try number three and pout, giving them the silent treatment (aloof and manipulative). Withdrawn into your own little world, you give occasional sideways glances to see if there's any weakening in your parent's resolve.

Realizing that being aloof has also failed to win them over to your side, you pull out your last option, strategy four, and mutter just loud enough to be heard, "You always get my brother what he wants . . . You don't love me" (poor-me or victim).

While these behaviors may seem all too familiar to parents, the interesting and somewhat troubling aspect to note is that most of us still use one of these control dramas as adults. Somewhere in our past, we tried one of these strategies and it worked and it became our go-to option for getting what we wanted.

Observing yourself, family, friends, or coworkers through the lens of control dramas can be revealing and insightful. However, the point is to recognize that control dramas and emotional reactivity are more likely in a mental environment overloaded with too much information. If we are unable to make our way through the morass of countless thoughts and mental jumble, our knee-jerk emotional reactions will override more mindful options for dealing with our moods and feelings.

- **Increased forgetfulness, misplaced items, accidents, and injuries:** A mind awash with too much information is a mind that isn't focused on the here and now. It becomes much more difficult to remember where you left your car keys, what you were about to say, or why you went into a room if your awareness is caught up in a swirl of unrelated thoughts and concerns. What's more, this hazy state of mind sets the stage for countless accidents and injuries. From minor dings and bumps, to tumbles, spills, and full-blown 911 emergencies, a lack of attention plays a huge role in making such incidents more likely. In the self-defense and martial arts community this is referred to as a lack of *situational awareness*. Simply put, situational awareness is the act of being engaged in our environment—awake, aware and noticing what's going on in our immediate vicinity. Sadly, this is not a state most of us find ourselves in frequently. Instead, we are either so totally immersed in our internal world or deeply absorbed in an external object (such as a cell phone) that we often put our safety in jeopardy.

On a related note, I find it interesting that in recent years our culture has seen a surge of interest in films and television programs depicting a zombie apocalypse. The irony is that the mental fog and distracted lifestyle we've been describing so far is in a way its own zombie apocalypse. Honestly, I find it a little sad seeing someone walking with their head down in their phone; not only is it unsafe, but they are missing out on so much of the world surrounding them. It makes me wonder, at the end of life, what will we each miss more—not being able to send one more text or scroll through our social media feed, or will it be to miss the sensation of fresh air filling our lungs, sunshine on our faces, and the earth beneath our feet?

> *A true zombie is nothing more than an unconscious being apathetically and lifelessly lumbering across the planet buying and consuming everything in its path, unsatisfied, unfulfilled, anxious and unstill.*
>
> —Judith Froemming

- **Relationship difficulties:** A successful relationship is only possible when both parties show up, meaning that each person in the relationship is engaged, attentive, and tuned in to the other. When we're distracted or overwhelmed with sensory and mental noise, we can't be genuinely receptive and supportive of our partner. We end up "phoning in" our relationship and are not present. This leads to missed opportunities, communication breakdowns, misunderstandings, arguments, and damage to the relationship on the whole.
- Lastly, and most obvious, is **a feeling of being overwhelmed and out of control:** Information overload creates a highly chaotic mental environment. This rapid (and routine) dump of data into our nervous system creates a feeling of being frazzled, anxious, and highly agitated. Inherently, we know this is not a healthy mental state to be in. We're like a swimmer caught in a rip current, struggling desperately to keep our head above water, while the current pulls us further out to sea. Unfortunately, it's a sad, but all-too-familiar experience for many of us on a daily basis. In particular, anxiety disorders have become increasingly common in our society. Like chronic worry on steroids, anxiety can have

a debilitating effect on our ability to function in our day-to-day lives.

I was unaware of the crippling effects of anxiety until recently. A few months ago, as my wife and I were carpooling on our way to work, we noticed a car pulled onto the shoulder of the opposite lane of traffic. The driver's door was open and a man was hanging out of the seat, half in, half out, apparently unconscious. I turned my car around and parked behind the vehicle so we could help the driver. While my wife called 911, I pulled the man fully into his seat and tried to determine his condition. He was barely conscious, breathing in short gasps, and clutching his chest with one hand while trying to dial his cell phone with the other. I am trained in CPR and felt certain the man was having a severe heart attack. My wife was able to redial the number he was trying to call on his phone and reached his wife to let her know what was happening. I did my best to keep the driver calm and slow his breathing for what seemed like an eternity until the EMTs arrived to take over. Once on the scene, they moved the driver to the ambulance so they could better assess his condition. A few minutes later (as my adrenaline rush was beginning to fade) the EMTs emerged to inform us that the man had apparently suffered an extreme anxiety attack. He would be fine, but they would be taking him to the hospital for observation. Good news for sure, but I was somewhat taken aback by their diagnosis and asked them about his symptoms of chest pain and shortness of breath. They told me that severe anxiety attacks (like this gentleman's) could cause crushing sensations in the chest, shortness of breath, and lightheadedness (in addition to the mental symptoms of extreme panic and alarm).

This was a sobering and eye-opening moment for me, to realize the severity and virtually incapacitating effects of anxiety on our well-being. Sadly, I fear that his man's experience is not that uncommon in the world today. Whether mild or extreme, the anxiety and mental tension brought on by profuse amounts of information, competing responsibilities and priorities, emotional turmoil, and the day-to-day pressures we all face can eat away at not only our happiness and peace of mind, but our ability to physically make it through the day in one piece.

So once again, we come to the end of a list of bad news bullet points and their subsequent effects on our mind-body system. We don't usually dissect the elements making up our state of *in*attention as we have done here, but I think it's helpful to understand the larger role these factors play on our mental stage. It can be somewhat disquieting, and perhaps even a little depressing, when we consider how the previously listed aspects contribute to our turbulent mind-space. Not to fear though, meditation comes to the rescue yet again, providing a host of unparalleled benefits to our brain, mind, and emotions. Read on . . .

YOUR BRAIN, MIND, AND EMOTIONS ON MEDITATION (MORE GOOD NEWS)

Now let's examine the effects of meditation on your brain, mind, and emotional state. To clarify—the brain, mind, and emotions are three distinct layers of our being that we often lump together out of convenience, but each represents a different level of mind-body function. The *brain* is the physical organ, and key structure of the central nervous system that governs all voluntary and automatic activity of our bodies. It's our central processor, command center, and focusing seat of intelligence and awareness. The *mind* is the repository of our sensory impressions. Combined with the intellect and ego, it forms what is known as the subtle body. This is the level we most intimately identify with, our sense of self, and the content of our thoughts. *Emotions* are mind-body states of feeling that are directly experienced rather than cognitively or intellectually reasoned. We don't *think* emotions; we *feel* them in the form of moods, sensations, and psychological changes. These separate, yet interwoven aspects of our being function together as part of the greater mind-body system while benefiting from meditation in their own unique ways.

Here are some of the things that happen at these levels during meditation:

- **Changes to the physical structure of the brain:** Research has demonstrated that individuals who practice meditation regularly are restructuring key areas of the brain. During a groundbreaking study in 2011, researchers at Massachusetts General Hospital used magnetic resonance imagery to measure key areas in the brains of sixteen study participants before and after they took part in an eight-week meditation program. In the analysis of the scans, researchers found an increased gray-matter density in key areas associated with learning, memory, self-awareness, compassion, and introspection in the meditators. Also discovered was a reduction in the gray-matter density in the amygdala, a part of the limbic system that plays an important role in anxiety and stress. Although this study is just the tip of the iceberg to understanding the specific mechanisms behind these changes, the implications are clear: meditation changes your brain's structure for the better in tangible and measurable ways.
- **Changes in brainwave activity:** Our brains produce different types of brainwaves during different activities and states of consciousness. For example, the:
  - » **Gamma brainwave state** (thirty to one hundred cycles per second) is a state of hyperactivity and active learning.
  - » **Beta state** (thirteen to thirty cycles per second) is the waking state, the working or thinking mind of analysis, planning, and rational thought.

- » **Alpha state** (nine to thirteen cycles per second) is a state of wakeful rest, relaxation, lucid and reflective thought.
- » **Theta state** (four to eight cycles per second) is the state of meditation, intuition, visualization, and expanded awareness.
- » **Delta state** (one to three cycles per second) is the state of deep, dreamless sleep.

So by practicing meditation, we are actually slowing down the frequency of our brainwaves and entering into the deeper theta state, expanding our capacity for wholeness.

- **Improves brain chemistry:** Our brains are constantly swimming in a unique blend of chemicals (neurotransmitters and hormones) that work to regulate and maintain our health and well-being. Meditation has been shown to positively influence our chemistry in several key ways:
  - » **Raises serotonin levels:** This happy or feel-good neurotransmitter has a crucial effect on our mood and lower serotonin levels can contribute to depression. Regular meditation helps to boost serotonin levels and maintain an optimal environment for the production of new brain cells.
  - » **Reduction in cortisol levels:** We've already looked at the damaging effects of cortisol on the body on the whole, but it is especially harmful to the brain. Neurologist and meditation teacher Dharma Singh Khalsa, MD, points out that "repeatedly subjecting the hippocampus to high levels of cortisol is almost like bathing the brain in battery acid." Fortunately, research has shown that meditators have a nearly 50 percent reduction in cortisol levels, thus helping to maintain a much healthier brain and nervous system.
  - » **Increased melatonin levels:** Melatonin is a key hormone associated with regulating restful sleep, strengthening the immune system, and slowing aging. Meditation has been shown to greatly enhance melatonin levels, perhaps serving as the

mechanism directly responsible for the improved sleeping patterns of regular meditators.
  » **Boosted dopamine levels:** The neurotransmitter dopamine regulates our pleasure-reward system and, when deficient, we can feel fatigued, unfocused, and unmotivated. Once again, meditation has demonstrated the ability to raise dopamine levels, increasing our feelings of enjoyment, happiness, and bliss.
  * Although these changes in brain chemistry are powerful and encouraging, please be sure to always consult your health care professional regarding changing any medication.

- **Enhanced brainwave coherence:** Coherence is another word for orderliness. Brainwave coherence is a basic indicator of how focused, organized, and holistically our brains are functioning. Most of the time, through our day-to-day activities, our brainwaves are firing hit and miss—scattered and rather disorganized. But meditation changes all that. It pulls everything together. Imagine going to a symphony. Before the concert begins, the members of the orchestra are warming up on their own, tuning their instruments, running scales, or rehearsing a few bars of music. It sounds sloppy, chaotic, and jumbled. But when the conductor comes to the podium and taps his baton, suddenly everything comes together and you hear a beautiful piece of music like Beethoven's Fifth Symphony. This is the effect meditation has on our brains. There is a synchronous "locking in" of disparate regions of the brain, and a unified order is established. This coherence is highly beneficial to overall brain function and is associated with increased learning ability, intelligence, creativity, self-control, and moral reasoning. In a nutshell, total and optimum brain functioning relies upon its coherence, and meditation powerfully contributes to this beneficial state.

- **Improved attention span:** Meditation helps to counteract the highly distracted and attention deficient state of mind we frequently find ourselves in, thereby creating a surplus of awareness. Through continually refocusing our attention on the mantra, breath, or similar anchor, we strengthen our ability to maintain one-pointed awareness. Just like lifting weights to strengthen our muscles, repeatedly bringing our attention back again and again, we forge new neurological pathways in our brains that grow stronger over time. This training conditions the mind to be less susceptible to wandering off and getting caught up in the next distraction. It's not unlike leash training a new puppy; in the beginning he's tugging you back and forth, stopping to sniff each tuft of grass, or jumping up on every passing stranger. But as you continue to guide him back to your side with gentle reassurance, he gains more and more discipline until he can stay focused and attentive to your direction without chasing after every passing squirrel. We do the same thing with our minds during meditation, gently and kindly bringing it back to the point of focus. It can take time and repeated effort, but eventually the new habit is formed and the ability to focus grows stronger.

Additionally, meditation helps to cultivate one of the eight limbs of yoga (more on this in the next chapter), known as *pratyahara*. Pratyahara is the act of temporarily withdrawing the senses from the outer world so we might deepen our connection to our inner voice and subtle senses. This "sensory fasting" happens to a greater or lesser degree each time we meditate; our eyes are closed, we're ideally in a quiet, physically comfortable environment, and are free from any noticeable aromas or tastes. In this state, our senses and their specific organs power down for a time, creating an opportunity to rest and not pull our attention in multiple directions. When we emerge from this period of pratyahara, we find that our sensory experiences are sharper, richer, more vibrant, and have opened us up a deeper perception of the world.

- **Increased neuroplasticity:** Neuroplasticity (*neuro* referring to the brain or nervous system, *plasticity* referring to flexibility) is the brain's ability to restructure itself by creating new neural connections and pathways throughout life. Ongoing research has begun to reveal that regular meditation has a significant effect on the brain's ability to grow new tissue. The brains of meditators show increased cortical thickness, increased gray-matter density in the brain stem, more gray matter in the hippocampus (associated with memory and learning), and white matter increases in parts of the brain connected to self-regulation. In a nutshell, this means that the brain is building additional connections in response to meditation. This is an important point as neuroplasticity is a crucial attribute in learning and developing new skills and abilities; neuroplasticity helps us continue to adapt and remain vital and mentally flexible as we age. Any new skill that we undertake, be it learning a musical instrument, a new language, a martial art, ballroom dancing, or cross-stitching, requires the formation of new neuro-networks. Those networks, through repeated use help the skill become increasingly instinctive and second nature. Enhanced neuroplasticity, facilitated by regular meditation, plays a key role in ensuring that our brains remain adaptive and malleable over the course of our lives.
- **Helps to override the negativity bias:** As we become more aware through meditation, we grow increasingly alert to a wider range of possibilities than our pre-programmed reactions of fear, anxiety, and negativity. Every situation contains infinite possibilities and interpretations; however, if we're not aware of those other choices, we continue to focus on only what we know. It's like having an unlimited variety of television channels to tune into, but because you don't know they exist, you continue to watch the same dismal and dreary reruns you been watching for months (or years). Once you expand your awareness, even just a little bit, you begin to realize that there were countless other programs and

you're no longer doomed to watch or react in the same unproductive manner. Seen in this way, the negativity bias is nothing more than a constriction in our awareness and with a slightly expanded vision we can choose to look for the good and positive in every moment.

- **Releases deeply stored psychological stress:** As we discussed in the previous chapter, mediation helps to greatly reduce stress and its effects on the physical body. However, meditation also significantly decreases *psychological* stress. The effects of stress don't reside only in the physical body; traumas, pent-up emotions, and unprocessed life experiences can get buried deep in our memories or repressed out of the reach of our conscious awareness. These hidden demons cling tightly to our inner world, often without us realizing that they are subtly influencing our choices and behavior. Fortunately, regular meditation can help to dislodge deeply stored mental and emotional stress. Like a gentle pressure washer, meditation slowly and over time peels away the layers of stress, tension, and anxiety trapped within us, eventually washing them away entirely. While our memories of those difficult issues may still remain, the negative emotional charge and stress will fall away. Sometimes people new to meditation ask if the same benefits couldn't also be accomplished by taking a long vacation, sitting in a hot tub, getting a massage, or lying on a quiet beach. While these options will undoubtedly reduce or eliminate the surface level of stress in your life, it's unlikely they will do much to remove the long-held stress that is stored at the deeper mental and emotional levels.

- **Decreases mental and emotional turbulence:** The settling effect of meditation on the mind helps to soothe the mental and emotional turbulence that is all too common in today's world. Even with the presence of thoughts during meditation, the frequency and strength of those thoughts is usually greatly reduced by the end of the session. The mantra's vibration persistently interrupting the stream of thoughts and emotions weakens their intensity from a powerful downpour to a light trickle, much in the same way a hurricane's strength is diminished when it makes landfall. What's more, that stillness often persists beyond the period of meditation and carries over into our daily activity. The calm and centered awareness we experience during meditation becomes the ground state of our being, a sanctuary that remains tranquil regardless of the turmoil outside its doors.

- **Reduced anxiety:** The endless stream of thoughts so typical of anxiety is lessened by meditation. Steady repetition of a mantra or the gentle refocusing of the mind on the breath helps to quiet the overactive brain, calming worrisome thoughts, and eventually allows our awareness to slip into the space between our thoughts. In that stillness, we begin to recognize that our thoughts, as important and critical as they may seem, are not who we really are. This dis-identification with our anxious and compulsive thoughts reduces their power to create so much chaos in our lives. Additionally, as we have seen, meditation can down-regulate the activity of the amygdala, which is the brain structure associated to emotions such as fear and anxiety. When the amygdala is less reactive, the resulting mental state is more clam and less prone to anxiety and panic.

- **Creates a sense of space or witnessing awareness:** This may be one of the most important benefits of meditation on the mental and emotional level. With regular practice we gradually become more attuned to an aspect of ourselves that stands apart and watches the world with detached awareness. This is often referred to as the witness or observer. This quality of our consciousness sits behind the scenes, seeing and hearing everything, just noticing without evaluation or judgment. In the absence of our regular inner critic, we experience a "spaciousness" or what Eckhart Tolle refers to as "space consciousness." In essence, there is a gap in which the stillness from meditation has begun to creep into our waking activity. In this space, we're able to stand back from the activity and drama in our lives and simply be aware, rather than getting caught up in the whole opera. The external turbulence calms and we are given an opportunity to pause, notice, and interrupt our automatically conditioned responses.

Connecting with this ever-present witnessing awareness contains enormous potential for mental and emotional well-being. So many of our life's difficulties can be attributed to making hasty or unconscious choices; we often fail to consider the impact of our thoughts, speech, or actions on ourselves or others. When we're able to slow down, stop, and notice what's going on in the present moment, we're much more likely to make more conscious, positive, and life-affirming choices. We let go of judgment and criticism and are more able to see the world as it really is, unclouded by our opinions and preconceived notions. This is a liberating experience and paves the way for lasting positive change in all areas of our lives. Holocaust survivor, neurologist, and psychiatrist Viktor Frankl, in his amazing book *Man's Search For Meaning* said, "Between stimulus and response there is a space. In that space is our power to choose our response. In our response lies our growth and our freedom." The space he is describing is the gap between our thoughts, a gap that is widened through the act of meditation.

This witnessing awareness also gives rise to one of meditation's deepest realizations—*you are not your thoughts*. This concept is so profound that it may take years to fully grasp. It also represents a significant shift away from how we have been conditioned to think about ourselves. If you think about it (and it may be something you've never considered before), you'll recognize that either consciously or unconsciously you fundamentally identify yourself with the *content* of your mind, in essence believing: I am my thoughts. Most of us completely accept this notion, contributing to the enormous power our thoughts have over us. When we believe our thoughts are us, we see them as absolute, unquestionable, infallible aspects of our being that we should take very personally—and seriously.

With the practice of meditation however, you start to recognize that rather than being the thought, you are the thinker of the thought. In and of themselves, thoughts are transient wisps of energy and information that come and go like autumn leaves. They have only the power you give them with repeated focus. As you bring your attention back to the mantra again and again, their influence over you weakens, eventually freeing you to use your thoughts instead of being used by them.

We'll explore the deeper meanings of who you are in future chapters. For now, just know that contained within this subtle shift away from identifying as your thoughts to the thinker of your thoughts lies a powerful secret for discovering the true nature of your mind.

- **Greater control over our emotions and choices:** As the witnessing awareness expands, we are able to have a pause, a moment or split second to actually notice what we're feeling, and respond consciously rather than reacting habitually. Without that space, we often end up on a kind of mental autopilot, thinking, behaving, and reacting as we always have through our familiar control dramas. But with the increased awareness that arises as a byproduct of meditation, we can notice when we are slipping into our old patterns. It can be insightful and transformative to witness your behaviors in the moment, especially if you catch yourself mindlessly resorting to old beliefs or programs. This act of self-course-correction can be thought of as yet another example of a mental *Jeet* or interception. In this case, however, what we are intercepting is ourselves and the old patterns of thinking and behaving that we are regularly activating. It's almost as if through meditation, we are able to slow down the events in the outside world long enough to interrupt and catch ourselves in the moment. From this space, we're much more able to make more nourishing and positive choices.

- **Access to higher states of insight, inspiration, and creativity:** While under the constant assault of stress, the centers of the brain associated with insight, creativity, and inspiration are stifled. The fight-or-flight response shunts blood flow away from the parts of the brain necessary to tap into new ideas and novel ways of thinking. However, with the return of the restful awareness kindled by meditation, those centers begin to come back to life, giving rise to imagination, ingenuity, and quantum jumps of creativity. Furthermore, the creative process itself is one that requires the incubation of information and data so it can be reshuffled, rearranged, and reimagined into something new that has never existed before. Meditation serves as the incubator for creativity, the cocoon from which a butterfly can emerge. So whether is a piece of music, a new scientific theory, a business project, or a recipe for an amazing meal, meditation helps to foster the state from which all new ideas can flow spontaneously.

- **Increased clarity of perception:** As the mind settles and the static of thought, beliefs, and preconceived notions begin to fall into the background, we gradually begin to experience an overall enhanced level of perception. In other words, we see the world, events, situations, relationships, and experiences from a much larger perspective. Where once we had seen just a narrow sliver of reality, we now start to perceive a much larger, deeply interrelated network of relationships, causes and effects, subtle intentions, and levels of awareness. We see the larger picture, the 30,000-foot view, which helps us understand and intuitively grasp the nature of how our minds works, how the world works, the hidden meanings behind events, and the patterns of energy, information, and consciousness that influence both our lives and the larger universe. It's as if we've been exploring a dark room with a flashlight, illuminating patches of artwork one at a time, only to discover once the lights are turned on that we've been inside the Sistine Chapel all along. Guided by this new awareness, the entire world becomes a fascinating playground of opportunities, a fantastic mystery, just waiting to be unmasked. As Aldous Huxley keenly observed, "There are things known and there are things unknown, and in between are the doors of perception." Meditation is a tool that allows us to cleanse our windows of perception, and in so doing we are able to see the world as it truly is.

As we can see from the foregoing list, meditation has the power to drastically alter the way our brains function, how we manage our emotions, and how we perceive the world. And this is just the beginning. I feel confident that in years to come the ongoing research on meditation will continue to reveal fascinating ways in which this practice affects our minds and emotions. Indeed, we may eventually come to recognize the literal truth behind French mathematician, physicist and religious philosopher Blaise Pascal's sentiment when he said, "All man's miseries derive from not being able to sit quietly in a room alone."

Hopefully these benefits have continued to demonstrate the value of incorporating a regular meditation practice into your life. But what if you want to look deeper still, beyond the mind, body, and emotions, to the realm of spirit, awareness, or consciousness? Well look no further, loyal reader. The next chapter is your stop.

> *As meditation deepens, compulsions, cravings, and fits of emotions begin to lose their power to dictate our behavior. We see clearly that choices are possible: we can say yes, or we can say no.*
>
> —Eknath Easwaran

CHAPTER 6

THE SPIRITUAL BENEFITS OF MEDITATION

I admit, I sometimes feel slightly uncomfortable when I begin to discuss the spiritual aspects of meditation. I think this is for two reasons. First, especially in a corporate setting, the emphasis is almost always on meditation as a tool for stress management, wellness, and increased productivity. Businesspeople aren't too concerned with ideas like "consciousness," "awareness," or "spirit"—at least not in the work environment. They're interested in the nuts and bolts of meditation—what it is, why it works, and what it can do for them (basically what the last few chapters have been about).

Second, I believe my uneasiness is also partially due to the fact that the idea of spirituality can be a concept that is both nebulous and also highly subjective. Spirituality means different things to different people and those personal beliefs can be guarded and delicate to navigate to avoid making people feel uncomfortable. I'm not here to tell anyone what to believe or force someone to question their long-held faith. Remember what I said in the beginning about being comfortable? Causing someone to doubt their religious convictions or fall headlong into a spiritual crisis would definitely be considered uncomfortable and is not what I'm after.

With that said though, in the context of this book, I feel more comfortable sharing with you in some detail the spiritual facets of meditation. I do this because I know from my own experience that there is great value in understanding this side of the practice. You're welcome to skip this chapter if you find the notion to be unpleasant or unappealing. However, I would strongly encourage you to push ahead with an open mind and explore, even if only briefly, this undiscovered territory.

WHY SPIRITUAL BENEFITS?

You may be thinking: What's the big deal about spiritual benefits? After all, perhaps you're like some of my business clients who are just trying to cut down on their stress. Why would you care about the relationship between meditation and spirituality? Well, there are several good reasons.

First, by looking at meditation's spiritual side it helps to make something that is somewhat abstract and esoteric more tangible and easier to understand. As I mentioned, for many people spirituality is a vague and hard-to-define concept. It can represent hard structured religious doctrine on one end of the spectrum and a fluffy, new-agey, woo-woo weirdness at the other. By breaking spirituality down, we'll have a better understanding of what it is and what it isn't.

Second, the ancient sages, seers, monks, and ascetics who developed the meditation techniques we use today didn't do so because life was stressing them out and they needed a way to relax. Meditation was devised by explores in consciousness and awareness. They wanted to understand the nature of reality: who they were, why they were here, what existence meant, and how to escape from suffering. Meditation was the tool, the means by which these pioneers were able to look within and answer life's biggest questions.

Therefore, meditation is technically a spiritual practice. It's part of the package. And while we in the West often somewhat strip-mine meditation away from its spiritual roots, the two aren't quite so easily separated. Yes, it's true, you can practice meditation as a purely secular mental technique, but meditation will always have a subtle spiritual component that is woven in at the deepest level.

This leads to the third point. Because spirituality is more or less "built-in" to meditation, understanding these benefits can help us be more aware of what we can expect as our practice progresses. It's like having a roadmap to a part of the country you've never driven through before; it gives us an idea of where the road leads and what we may see along the way, as well as how to avoid the pitfalls and dead ends we may encounter.

Lastly, since I'm dedicated to giving you a well-rounded understanding and respect for meditation, I feel it's important for you to be familiar with the whole picture. Spiritual growth is a natural byproduct of a regular meditation practice, and by spiritual growth, I simply mean the expansion of awareness. Perhaps you don't consider that to be spiritual. Perhaps you do. Regardless, by exploring this aspect of meditation, you'll be able to have a more complete understanding of the practice.

WHAT DOES IT MEAN TO BE SPIRITUAL?

Let's break this down. What does spirituality mean? Although spirituality is a personal and subjective experience, which prevents it from being defined by the normal methods of scientific investigation, it does have some recognizable qualities that can help it feel a little more concrete and solid.

First, spirituality is not defined by religious belief. You can be spiritual without following a specific faith or doctrine. We may know someone, perhaps ourselves, who identifies as spiritual, but *not religious*. Spirituality does not require that you subscribe to an organized belief system or ideology. It is free of institutions and hierarchies and focuses on the manner in which we view the world, our attitudes toward it, practices for exploring our place in it, and discovering the values we hold to be meaningful. It is sometimes thought of as a "search for the sacred" or a means to experience our "higher self," both of which can happen independently of a formal establishment or structure.

Next, spirituality leans toward a universal, all-embracing worldview rather than an exclusive or absolute ideology. It favors inclusivity over exclusivity. Everyone is welcome on the path, not just certain people who have a fixed set of beliefs. As Krishna reminds his disciple in the *Bhagavad Gita*: "As men approach me, so I receive them. All paths Arjuna, lead to me."

This paints the picture of no one right way to spiritual truth. There are many paths up the mountain. We are all welcome to undertake the journey on whatever route we choose.

Spirituality is about experience rather than belief. In this regard, it could be considered the path of the mystic in which one seeks to have a direct experience of truth, the divine, or higher states of consciousness instead of reading or studying about the experiences of others. This is about making direct and personal contact with the nature of reality. It's a call to go beyond our personal beliefs to discover for ourselves firsthand who we truly are.

Spirituality also favors *love over fear*. Let's be honest, there are quite a few religions and belief systems that put an emphasis on fear—fear of going against God's will, fear of divine judgment, fear of eternal damnation, fear of losing the approval of the tribe, institution, or organization. These fears can lay the groundwork for a terrifying, guilt- and anxiety-riddled worldview. However, a worldview based upon spirit is one in which the values of love, compassion, forgiveness, and implicit worth are extended to all beings, everywhere.

Going further, spirituality's expansive state fosters a deeper connection with all of life and all the forms it takes. Vedanta reminds us that from a spiritual perspective: God is not hard to find, he is impossible to avoid. If spirit is an all-encompassing field of consciousness or awareness, then by definition there is nowhere that it is not. It includes everything and everyone; animal, plant, mineral, down to the smallest microbe or subatomic particle. When you realize that the world is your extended body, it becomes apparent that the separation we often feel is the result of a fragmented and constricted worldview.

Next, being spiritual is about being self-referral. Self-referral means that in order to know ourselves we look within. We define who we are based upon internal guidance and criteria. Our internal reference point is the ever-present witnessing awareness at the core of our being. It's a connection to true power that allows us to feel independent of the good or bad opinions of others, above no one and beneath no one, and fearless in the face of change. It is our true identity. The opposite of self-referral is object-referral in which our internal reference point is externals—our ego, our positions and possessions, our status, and sense of approval from others. Object-referral is false power—impermanent and fleeting. Self-referral is the eternal, unbounded state of our true nature.

Spirituality also has the quality of fostering inner understanding as opposed to outer worship. Instead of putting our attention on something outside of ourselves for knowledge or wisdom, we explore and trust the intuitive voice that comes from within. This further develops the qualities of introspection, self-inquiry, and contemplation. If you're beginning to notice a pattern here, it's no coincidence; the spiritual experience is an *inward journey*. Or as Marcel Proust puts it: "The real voyage of discovery consists, not in seeking new landscapes, but in having new eyes."

This means that spirituality is about living life in a more reverent or sacred manner. With the world as our body, we live a life of gratitude, in a state of constant amazement, marveling at the miracle of our own existence. We enjoy life more, and we have less anxiety over how long it will last.

Last, spirituality doesn't mean that we have to retreat from the world by running away to a mountain cave, ashram, or monastery. Spirituality can be experienced right here, right now, regardless of your lifestyle, where you live, or what you do. In more traditionally religious societies, there were two paths available to a spiritual aspirant: the ascetic or the householder. The path of the ascetic meant renouncing the world in order to completely dedicate oneself to spiritual matters. Free from the daily grind of chores, family, work, and societal responsibilities, a monk or yogi could commit all their time and energy to spiritual practice.

The path of the householder was exactly the opposite. The householder remained in the world performing their regular duties with family and personal relationships while simultaneously engaging in a spiritual life and practice. If you had to guess, which of these two paths would you think is more difficult? Some might believe that giving up everything to pursue a spiritual calling might be the more extreme way to go, but as someone who has been on the path of the householder for many years now, I find it can be quite a challenge to live a spiritual life while working full time, teaching, being a husband, paying bills, and tending to countless daily responsibilities. That, however, is not meant to scare you off. I presume that you fall into this category as well, but take heart—being a householder on a spiritual path provides *so many* opportunities to deepen our practice and explore the spiritual dimension of our lives in ways that might not be available to us if we renounced the world to go live in a cave. These opportunities, this endurance event that is our daily experience provides us with what Ram Dass called *grist for the mill*—the raw material that will be used to convert us into more awakened beings.

So these are the qualities of spirituality. If I had to boil them down into a simple, concise definition it would be this: Living life in a more awakened, aware, and deeply genuine and present manner. Now that we understand spirituality, let's take a closer look at the role meditation plays in this process.

THE SPIRITUAL BENEFITS OF MEDITATION

At this point you may be thinking, "Oh great, another long list of meditation benefits and statistics." If that's the case, you'll be happy to know that in this section we're only going to focus on two spiritually related meditation benefits. Maybe that comes a disappointment for some of you. Perhaps you were expecting supernormal powers, clairvoyance, ESP, bilocation, astral projection, levitation, telepathy, communing with the dead, or remote viewing. While all those phenomena could be considered interesting and worthy of exploration, they're a little more along the lines of the external special effects we discussed in Chapter 2, rather than a clue that true transformation is taking place. According to the wisdom tradition of Vedanta, there are just two indicators that your life is moving in a spiritual direction, two signposts that help you see you're on the road to higher consciousness. They are as follows.

1. **An Increasing Sense of *Lightheartedness*:** One of the most pleasant byproducts of a regular meditation practice is that you begin to experience an increased feeling of carefreeness, lightness, and joy. Life doesn't feel so heavy or burdensome. There is less worry and anxiety, less obsessive compulsive thinking and acting. We find ourselves less concerned with where we're going, and more content to enjoy the journey. We're not as preoccupied with how long life will last and more content with simply enjoying it while we're here. Judgment diminishes, our demands on self and others are lessened, and serenity in the present moment becomes an increasingly regular experience.

    In this expanding lightheartedness, we find ourselves taking life much less seriously. This often comes as a huge relief for our mind and body. Consider for a moment how seriously most of us take ourselves. Why shouldn't we? After all, life in the modern world is a terribly serious business. We take our sense of self seriously; we take our body, name, title, and job seriously; we take our possessions seriously; we take our relationships seriously;

we take the contents of our minefield seriously; we even take our lane on the highway seriously. All this seriousness creates an enormous mental, emotional, and spiritual burden for us to carry day in and day out. It can be exhausting being so serious all the time.

I recall a story Dr. David Simon told of a meditation retreat guest who was passionate about finding someone to spend her life with. She told David, "More than anything, I want to be in a serious relationship." David paused at the question, smiled and said, "But why would you want a *serious* relationship? There's nothing less enjoyable than a serious relationship. Why wouldn't you want a lighthearted relationship, a playful relationship, joyful relationship?"

Think back to when you were a small child. Was life so serious then? Of course not. You were all bubbles, giggles, curiosity, lightheartedness, and joy. You weren't all solemn and grim; you were happy, loving, and—dare I say—blissful. That's the true nature of a child. We were all there at one time. "But wait," you say. "Children don't have the responsibilities adults have." That's true, they don't, but having responsibilities does not equate to a doleful and somber existence. It's the *interpretation* of those responsibilities that determines if we react to them with dread or joy, and meditation changes that interpretation.

When we become less serious, we're much less inclined to be offended by people, events, and situations. Taking offense or feeling slighted is a result of our identification with the *ego*, our false sense of self. The more we cling to that little self, the more easily offended we will be. When we tap into the self-referral quality of our spirit or soul, however, ego concerns have less control over our lives. Rather than being triggered by the behavior of others or external events we are able to step back and remember our ego is just the role we are playing, not our true self. With that understanding comes liberation from feeling disrespected or affronted by the world. We can laugh at ourselves knowing that few situations are worth losing our peace of mind over.

With meditation we have more fun, we enjoy life more. We begin to recognize how fragile, beautiful, amazing, silly, paradoxical, and miraculous it is to find ourselves aware and awake in a body that began when sperm met egg, on small planet, orbiting an average star, one of billions in a galaxy surrounded by countless others. When the veil of stress lifts we can begin to grasp our place in this universe; in so doing, it is impossible not to be filled with a sense of wonder, reverence, awe, and gratitude for our unique speck of awareness that looks out into the world. There's a quote in one of my favorite movies, *Joe Versus the Volcano*, that sums up this experience beautifully: "My father says that almost the whole world is asleep. Everybody you know. Everybody you see. Everybody you talk to. He says that only a few people are awake and they live in a state of constant, total amazement."

In this state of constant and total amazement it's nearly impossible not to feel happy. In fact, happiness and bliss are our natural state. Unfortunately, they are overshadowed so much of the time by our stress, anxiety, and mental and emotional turbulence, that we forget they're there. As meditation peels away those layers of static our true nature can emerge, like the sun from behind a cloud. That happiness becomes our ground state and even during "serious" times, we can see things from a more lighthearted perspective. If you've ever seen videos of the Dalai Lama, Maharishi Mahesh Yogi, Mother Teresa, Paramahansa Yogananada, or one of the countless modern sages of India, they seem to smile constantly, laugh or giggle frequently, and have a carefree and easygoing sense of themselves and their place in the world. Despite doing important, even earth-changing work for the betterment of the world, they don't get all caught up in the drama or their sense of self-importance. They enjoy the role they are playing without getting overwhelmed by it. They know they are in this world but not of it; here for a short time to embrace this human experience fully and passionately, with lightness of being.

Q: Why do angels fly?

A: Because they take themselves *lightly*.

2. **Experiencing the Spontaneous Fulfillment of Desire:** The second spiritual benefit to a regular meditation practice is what can be known as the spontaneous fulfillment of desire, or put more simply, the effortless manifestation of your intentions into physical reality. For some, this idea suggests a descent from reason into the realm of "magical thinking" in which our thoughts can bring about effects in the external world. However, what I'm proposing here doesn't necessarily imply some spooky otherworldly powers, just simply the fact that life becomes *easier and more effortless*.

Have you ever watched a sporting event and one player, perhaps Michael Jordan for example, was just *on fire*, performing nearly flawlessly, in synch with his team, moving almost effortlessly and without resistance? Or if you've ever watched a Bruce Lee film you've witnessed the incredible flow of his water-like movements, seeking their target with least effort, using the minimal amount of energy to organically slice through his opponents as if in a dance. In these situations, we say that person was "in the zone," a state of deeply interconnected, present-moment awareness in which they are so in tune with the music of their environment that they are perfectly positioned to capitalize on each opportunity as it arises. These individuals appear to be good-luck magnets, drawing to themselves exactly what they needed in that moment to fulfill their intentions.

However, good luck is nothing but preparedness and opportunity coming together. Our preparedness comes from the practice of meditation which helps to remove the blockages from our mind and body that would obscure our awareness from recognizing the opportunities in each moment.

In this way we can paradoxically accomplish more by doing less. We increasingly begin to find ourselves in just the right place at the just right time to more easily fulfill our desires. Our intentions seem to have a mind of their own, and what we put our attention on has an unseen influence on what continues to show up in our lives. At times it may feel as if the entire universe is colluding and plotting to take your life in the direction of your dreams and aspirations. To use a video game analogy, it's as if through the practice of meditation we are given the cheat codes that rig the game of life in our favor.

When this happens, we experience more coincidence, synchronicity, and the miraculous. If you think *miracle* too strong a word, consider that it literally means "to wonder at, marvel, or be astonished." When these experiences begin to happen, and they will with the regular and dedicated practice of meditation, it becomes difficult not to be filled with wonder at the extreme improbability of their existence through rational means. The mind boggles at the manner in which a unique set of events or circumstances came into being—knowing deep down that even with the help of a think tank of experts, a super computer, and a slide-rule we couldn't have planned or organized the outcome to that degree.

The term synchronicity was first coined by the Swiss psychologist Carl Jung to describe the connection between two or more *acausal* (not causally related) events. Synchronicity is not a simple, senseless coincidence, but rather one that is significant and breaks through from the unconscious to the conscious realm saying, "Hey, pay attention to this!" These moments are so unlikely that they cause a spike in our attention and create an opportunity to more easily fulfill a desire or lead our lives in a new direction.

I've had several of these experiences in my life over the years, and I'd like to share two of them with you. The first took place in 1997. I had just completed my first week-long meditation retreat in Ashville, North Carolina. At the end of the retreat, we were instructed to continue our regular meditation and be on the lookout for synchronicities as hints that our practice was deepening. Following the final session, I hopped in my car and began the drive from North Carolina to my parent's home in Western Pennsylvania, where I would be a groomsman in a good friend's wedding.

The drive led me from North Carolina through Virginia and West Virginia into Pennsylvania. The route I had chosen (before the days of GPS phone apps) took me on a mix of interstate highways and rural roads. One of those small roadways cut through the quiet West Virginia countryside. I must have been caught up in my music or still accustomed to the higher speed of travel from the highway I had recently exited to realize I was traveling over the posted speed limit. I looked into my rearview mirror, saw the flash of police lights, and felt the not so pleasant fight-or-flight cascade we explored in Chapter 3.

The state trooper approached my car and explained that I had been pulled over for driving 65 mph in a 55-mph zone. He asked for my license, registration, and insurance and headed back to his car to, I assumed, write me a ticket. A few minutes later, another trooper arrived and began talking to the other. Although standard police procedure, it made me more nervous knowing that I had a three-hour drive to go; I wanted to be on my way.

The second trooper approached and asked a few additional questions about my destination and if I had any weapons with me before returning to his car to call in my license. Finally, the trooper returned and said, "Mr. Brady, you were pulled over for going 65 in a 55-speed zone, which is a ticketable offense. . ." I sighed and waited for him to hand me my ticket. "However," he continued, "It turns out that today is the first day that the speed limit on this roadway is changing from 55 miles per hour to 65 miles per hour. So, you're free to go."

"Whut?" I said.

"You're free to go. Drive safe."

He handed me back my license and I sat somewhat perplexed in my car before slowly pulling back onto the road for the uneventful remainder of my drive.

The second experience of synchronicity took place in 2004. When I was still dating my then future wife, we took a trip to visit her father who lived in Philadelphia. During our visit the three of us decided to go into the city and see some of the historic sites. After viewing the Liberty Bell and Benjamin Franklin's home, we made our way to Independence Hall. I was excited to see the home of the Second Continental Congress because 1) in college I had played Thomas Jefferson in the musical *1776*, which took place in Independence Hall when the Declaration of Independence was being written and signed, and 2) I've always had an affinity for and been fascinated by America's Revolutionary War period.

We had called ahead to learn that while there was no charge to enter Independence Hall, tickets were still required and only a limited number were issued each day. Sadly, we got to the ticket window just in time to learn that they had given out the last tickets of the day. I was bummed. I had really wanted to see the inside of this piece of our nation's history. So instead, we settled on visiting the continental library, which stands right next to Independence Hall.

My wife needed to use the restroom before we went in, so her father and I waited outside so we could all go in together. While we waited, he and I chatted about the history of the area and what it must have been like to live in those times. I looked to the ground and noticed a few pieces of paper on the cobblestones and automatically bent down to pick them up. (I'm the product of a theme park culture that conditions people to compulsively pick up trash as if by no will of their own.) I flipped the three slips of paper over to read the following words: Entrance to Independence Hall—Admit One Adult.

I stared, gob-smacked into my hand for a full ten seconds before looking around the square. I figured someone must have dropped the tickets or I was being filmed by *Candid Camera*. However, no one else was nearby. It was as if the tickets just "showed up" for the three of us. It was then that I remembered that I had just recently begun reading a new book on advanced meditation techniques and synchronicity. I showed the tickets to my now father-in-law who shockingly said, "Where did you get those?" I explained that they had been right under our feet all along. He too was shocked. My wife joined a few moments later and we told her the story to which she replied, "Oh that kind of thing happens to you all the time."

I share these stories to illustrate the inexplicable way that events can flow and more easily lead to the fulfillment of desires brought about through the practice of meditation. I believe that these incidents were the result of the conspiracy of improbabilities—an environment of enhanced likelihood that things will move in the direction you have intended. And that conspiracy of improbabilities is cultivated specifically through meditation. With increased awareness comes openness, a receptivity to these spikes of improbability and what they mean. We begin to sense the interconnectedness and entanglement of all things and it opens the door to the miraculous in our lives.

Sure, skeptics could probably run the odds of a speeder dodging a ticket the day the speed limit changes while driving home following a meditation retreat that helps to cultivate synchronicity. Or the chance that three non-existent Independence Hall tickets would drop into my hand within days of starting to explore synchronicity meditation techniques. But for one, those odds would be staggering, and two, the impact of such events can only be understood within the unique subjective context of meaning for that person. Remove any of the key components and it becomes *meaningless* coincidence. The human element is what gives synchronicity its significance and allows the spontaneous fulfillment of desire to flourish.

Maybe it seems too hard to believe. Maybe it doesn't jive with how you think the world operates. That's okay. Today's miracle is tomorrow's science. Dissecting a miracle doesn't make it any less wondrous; what matters is the experience. So rather than dismissing this benefit of meditation out of hand, I suggest you take a step into the unknown, commit to a regular meditation practice, be open and awake to coincidences, follow their clues, and see where they lead.

MEDITATION AND THE FIELD OF CONSCIOUSNESS

Until this chapter, we've been discussing meditation from a relatively materialistic perspective. In other words, we've been looking at the nuts and bolts of how meditation works in the real world of our bodies, health, minds, emotions, and so on. In this section, however, we're going to venture into the not-so-tangible, not-so-measurable realm of consciousness itself. This is an area of study that many of us not only don't regularly think about, but we literally don't know *how* to think about it. This discussion may be a little challenging to follow, and perhaps sound a little far-fetched, but I assure you, it relates directly back to our practice of meditation and has implications that could literally change the world. So buckle up and prepare to explore a fascinating new worldview.

First off, exactly what do I mean by consciousness? In its most simple definition, *consciousness* is "the quality or state of being aware, especially of something within oneself." It's essentially awareness of our own awareness. You are conscious, I am conscious; we know we are aware and have a subjective experience of that awareness. But unlike other qualities of the material universe, it's not something we can touch, point to, or quantify. Consciousness is something we know we have, but in many ways that's about all we know. Where does consciousness come from? What are its properties? How can we study it? The Australian philosopher and cognitive scientist David Chalmers has called consciousness *the hard problem* because understanding the nature of consciousness is exceedingly difficult in that we can't readily explain why consciousness exists or what physical mechanism brings it about. As we try to probe its mysteries, consciousness becomes even more mysterious and tricky.

Fundamentally, there are two theories on the origins of consciousness.

1. Consciousness is entirely physical and is a byproduct of the brain. That is to say at a certain level of evolution a critical complexity threshold was crossed and viola! Consciousness! Our awareness is then the end result of a complicated arrangement of atoms and molecules that eventually learned to think, and therefore think about themselves.
2. The second theory is that rather than being the after-effect of highly evolved brains, consciousness is instead the fundamental ground state of the universe. In this view, consciousness underlies

and gives rise to all the energy, information, and material "stuff" of the universe. In essence, this means that the ultimate state of the universe is consciousness itself. Beneath all the stars and galaxies, planets, oceans, continents, cities, buildings, cars, people, dogs, trees, blades of grass, and even rocks lies an infinite ocean of awareness.

As it turns out, this second theory is curiously aligned with some of the world's great wisdom traditions and will be the foundations of our exploration going forward. Remember our discussion on yoga from Chapter 1? The practice of yoga is about the philosophy, the insights and techniques that help us to experience the *union* of our local selves with the larger, non-local self of the universe. That non-local self is the underlying field of consciousness at the heart of all creation.

> *"It's a remarkable fact that the people who have gone the very deepest into the mind—the sages and saints of every religious tradition—all say essentially the same thing: your fundamental nature is pure, conscious, peaceful, radiant, loving, and wise, and it is joined in mysterious ways with the ultimate underpinnings of reality, by whatever name we give That."*
> —Rick Hanson, *Buddha's Brain: The Practical Neuroscience of Happiness, Love, and Wisdom*

But how can this be? It all comes down to the three levels of reality: material, mental, and spiritual. Over the course of our lifetimes most of us have developed a strictly material bias when looking at the world around us. We experience life exclusively through our five senses, assuming that the hard and solid stuff of the universe is all there is.

However, nearly a century ago the pioneers of quantum physics revealed that the material model of the world only described a partial picture of a much larger universe. An entirely new layer of reality existed far beyond the threshold of what our senses could perceive. This was the level of energy and information, and the domain of the mind. But even deeper still was the presence of an underlying field of awareness that seemed to be influenced by the thoughts and expectations of the scientists exploring these realms, leading them to conclude that consciousness itself was a primary component of the reality they were studying.

These three levels or reality are closely mirrored in the yoga philosophy through what is known as the *layers of life*. This model was first mapped out by the legendary Vedic Sage, Adi Shankara. Born a child prodigy in the eighth century AD, Shankara was said to speak fluent Sanskrit at an early age, became well versed in the Vedic literature and practice through childhood, and was teaching and giving his own commentaries on the Vedas in his teens. Prior to taking *mahasamadhi* (the great and final meditation during which the yogi leaves their body through conscious death) in his early thirties, Shankara established four schools of learning in India (East, West, North, and South) to help spread his philosophy and interpretation of Vedanta known as *advaita* or "non-dualism."

This philosophy essentially is meant to correct the fundamental error of the intellect that creates divisions and separations where none actually exist. It teaches that, as we've already discussed, everything in existence is unity or oneness. However, the non-local consciousness splits itself up into an infinite variety of forms and phenomena to create a multitude of perspectives from which to observe itself. It's as if consciousness is playing an elaborate game of hide and seek, disguising itself in every person, animal, tree, plant, mountain, planet, or galaxy. Shankara's model of the layers of life presents us with a way to better understand the forms consciousness takes so we can more easily grasp the underlying unity behind each division. Each layer is known as a *kosha*, meaning the sheath or covering that veils the true self. Shankara describes three primary layers that consist of three additional sublayers. Let's take a closer look at each level.

- **The First Layer—The Physical Body**
  This is the level of material reality we are most familiar with. It consists of the field of atoms and molecules that comprise every "hard" or "solid" object in our existence. Its three sublayers are: the extended body or the environment, the personal body, and the energetic body.
  1) **Extended Body or Environment:** Even though we may feel separate and detached from our surroundings, there is no distinct boundary between ourselves and the rest of the universe. Our bodies are in a state of constant communication with the outside world. Through our pores and lungs, we exchange billions of atoms of air with the environment. We are nourished by water and food that come from the earth's extended body of plants and animals. The cycles and rhythms of nature influence our minds and bodies at subtle levels. Our five senses are the gateways through which we are in constant communication with the world, taking in all manner of external influences. At every level, we are woven into the tapestry of the environment in which we live.
  2) **Personal Body:** Called the *annamaya* kosha or "the covering made of food", this is the layer of life represented by our individual physical body. Comprised of cells, tissues, organs, systems, bones, and muscles, the annamaya kosha is our personal vehicle within which our consciousness resides throughout our lifetime. We often consider it to be our most intimate experience of "mine." This layer is also a reflection of the type and quality of experiences we digest: food, toxins, stress, rest, etc.

3) **Energetic Body:** Known in Sanskrit as *pranamaya* kosha, this is the sheath or covering of vital, primordial life-energy. Prana is the life force that separates a healthy and vibrant human being from a lifeless corpse. It animates and vitalizes every system in our bodies giving rise to boundless energy, enthusiasm, creativity, and movement. Although there are five seats of prana in the human body, we receive most of this vital life force form the food we eat and the air we breathe. The pranayama kosha is equivalent to the electromagnetic field or aura that resonates through and around our physical form.

- **The Second Layer—The Subtle Body or Mind Field**

Beyond the physical level, we arrive at the mental layers of life. The subtle body comprises the mind-space with which we regularly identify as "me." The three secondary layers are divided into mind, intellect, and ego.

1) **Mind:** The *manomaya* kosha. In this model, the mind is the repository of our sensory impressions. All the perceptions of our five senses are recorded at this level. These impressions can be described as *qualia*, or the indivisible instances of subjective conscious experience. The "red" of a rose or the "sound of a church bell" generate a characteristic *feel* that gets stored away at this layer of life. These impressions are also influenced by our mental states. Moods, emotions, or states of consciousness color our sensory perceptions, giving them a unique and subjective texture.

> *I believe in what I see*
> *I believe in what I hear*
> *I believe that what I'm feeling*
> *Changes how the world appears*
>
> —Totem, Neil Peart/Rush

2) **Intellect:** The *buddhimaya* kosha is the mental layer from which we judge, evaluate, discriminate, and critically examine the contents of our experience. Through analysis and reason, the intellect scrutinizes the sensory content of the mind to make appropriate choices. It studies, compares, and appraises all mental input in an attempt to distinguish the *unreal* from the *real*. The intellect can be a powerful ally in understanding and making sense of the world we live in; however, its churning activity can generate a great deal of mental turbulence and static if not balanced with periods of stillness.

3) **Ego:** In the yoga philosophy, the ego is known in as *ahankara* or "the I-former." It is our most intimate identity of I, me, my, and mine. The ego is our object-referred state, associated with our positions, possessions, self-importance, and need for approval and recognition. It embodies our sense of being separate, special, and better than others. Of all the layers of life, the ego is the most constricted and pinched off from the flow of spirit. However, the ego isn't necessarily bad or evil; it's just another mask that consciousness wears to keep itself guessing. Seen for what it is, we can allow it to be without getting trapped by its drama.

The mind field is subtly at play in all you do. For example, when you go to the movies and walk into the theater, your *mind* first takes in all the sensory impressions or sounds, slights, people, etc. Next, the *intellect* becomes engaged when you evaluate, consider, and determine where you want to sit. Lastly, after you have sat down and settled into the seat, your *ego* tags the location as "my personal seat."

- **The Third Layer—The Causal Body**

"Causal" means acting as a cause of, or giving rise to; therefore, this deepest layer is the realm of spirit from which the mind and body arise. This is the field of pure consciousness, pure creativity that gives birth to the manifest universe. It, too, has three sublayers.

1) **Personal Soul:** This is the individualized component of the field of spirit, our personal soul made up of all our unique choices, memories, and desires. It's like our spiritual fingerprint, a unique wave on the infinite ocean of consciousness. In Sanskrit, this aspect of our sprit is called the *Atman*; it is the ever-present witnessing awareness that we contact in the stillness of meditation. Since the potency of unbounded awareness is so vast and infinite, our personal soul acts like a step-down transformer to regulate its power and energy to a usable form in our human experience. Yet, despite being scaled-down to a manageable level, our personal soul still maintains the fundamental characteristics of the universal soul:

   » Non-local: Your soul doesn't have a specific time-space address; it's not simply in your body, in heaven, or behind the couch. It is in all places and at all times. It is everywhere in general and nowhere in particular. It can't be restricted to any one location or time. As Jesus says in the Gospel of Thomas, verse 77: "Split a piece of wood, and I am there. Lift up a stone, and you will find Me there."

   » Acausal, or without a cause: Your soul has always been and always shall be. It is infinite, immortal, undying. In the *Bhagavad Gita*, Krishna reminds Arjuna that the soul is unbreakable and incombustible; it can neither be dampened nor dried. It is everlasting, in all places, unalterable, immutable, and primordial.

   » Existing at the deepest level of reality: Since your soul is everywhere, it permeates the finest level of the universe. Down to the smallest subatomic particles—and beyond our mind's ability to even grasp—is a domain your soul calls home.

» Interconnected to everything: Being all places and times, your soul is threaded through and interrelated to everything and everyone in existence. In Vedanta, there is the metaphor of *Indra's Net*, in which the universe exists as an infinite web spread in all directions without beginning or end. Wherever strands of the web intersect, there is a jewel that reflects all other jewels. In the same way, your soul exists in an entangled relationship with all other souls, separate and unique, yet deeply intertwined.

2) **The Collective Soul:** This is the layer in which groups of personal souls resonate together, creating group consciousness. This is similar to the way in which heart cells work together to beat your heart or stomach cells digest food. Individuals vibrating at certain frequencies of consciousness are drawn together for a specific purpose. These patterns of consciousness embody the motifs, themes, and archetypal energies of great myths, gods and goddesses, heroes and villains, saints and damned. These energies seek out expression in each of us so they may be played out on both the world stage and our individual lives. Archetypes and collective themes pull at us to live lives of heroic proportions as we fulfill our purpose in life.

3) **The Universal Soul:** This is both the deepest and most expansive layer of our being. At this level of pure consciousness, the universe is unmanifest; in other words, it has no qualities of its own, yet it brings forth the whole of manifest creation. This is the infinite ocean of spirit beyond all duality or divisions, total unity consciousness in which our individual soul is merged back into the universal self—the infinite potential of all that was, all that is, and all that ever will be. Beyond the countless expressions the ocean can take, *it's all water*, creating itself again and again. At this layer of consciousness, we can see that everything is within. We are the director, the actor, the

scenery, the special effects, the music, the projector, and the screen; we're the whole movie. The great saying, or *mahavakya* in Sanskrit is *tat tvam asi*, which means: "I am that!"

Armed with this additional understanding, it becomes increasingly clear how the layers of life map onto the three layers of reality (matter, mind, and spirit). We are not simply bags of skin that learned how to think. We are multilayered beings that are deeply interwoven into the infinite field of consciousness.

During meditation our awareness travels through all the layers of life and the entire range of consciousness. We meditate in a specific location that is part of the extended body or environment, we settle into our personal body as the vehicle for our practice, as we begin to repeat the mantra, we create a vibration that enlivens our prana or energetic body; our senses settle and withdraw allowing our mind to become quiet, the intellect loosens its grip on discursive thinking and evaluations, the sense of self or I fades into the background; and we step outside the ego's tiny confines, embracing the fullness of our personal soul, the unique expression of spirit we represent. Expanding further, we embody the whole of humanity's story and our role in it, until finally our awareness steps into the infinite unboundedness of pure awareness.

We are consciousness. The universe is consciousness. Everything is consciousness. This concept is vital to our understanding going forward. If everything is consciousness, we are essentially *all the same thing in different disguises*. We're all connected, interrelated, entangled, and unified together as one. Our sense of separateness is a leftover artifact of perception. We're all threads in the fabric of the cosmos. Therefore, we arrive at a simple and elegant conclusion: what one of us does affects the whole field of consciousness.

Pluck one string and the entire web shakes.

MEDITATION AND GLOBAL TRANSFORMATION

If consciousness is then the ground state of the universe, the underlying field of awareness at the heart of reality, we have to rethink our practice of meditation. Remember the discussion in Chapter 4 on the effects meditation had on increasing brainwave coherence? That coherence or orderly harmony isn't just localized to our brainwaves, it is felt by every cell in the body. The heart, in particular, has a close relationship with the brain and its orderly function. According to research performed by the Institute of HeartMath, when someone is experiencing deeply positive emotions such as love or appreciation their brainwaves and heart rate variability (an indicator of overall heart health and nervous system function) become "entrained" or closely synchronized. Essentially, the heart and head are having on ongoing conversation about our perceptions, thoughts, and emotions and when we're in a deeply settled, peaceful, and coherent state we experience it at every level of our being.

But it doesn't stop there. The heart generates a powerful electromagnetic field (the pranamaya kosha) that envelops our entire body and extends like a large donut approximately eight to ten feet into the space around us. This field is not just simple energy, rather it's an important carrier of subtle energetic information encoded and modulated within the rhythm of our heartbeat. We are in fact, broadcasting the content of who we are, how we feel, our moods, emotions, and states of mind out into the surrounding environment. When we are at peace, we radiate peace into our surroundings; when we are angry, violent, or hostile, we similarly transmit those subtle energy signatures into the world around us. In the words of Ralph Waldo Emerson, "Who you are shouts so loudly in my ears, I can't hear what you're saying."

As you can see, therefore, we are never acting, thinking, speaking, or feeling in a vacuum. We are constantly affecting the collective consciousness with our thoughts, emotions, intentions, and states of mind. What's more, our fields are interacting with the fields of others, subtly influencing and being influenced by their states of consciousness.

Here's where it gets really interesting. As we meditate our individual coherence increases, which is then projected into the surrounding environment. But when groups of people come together to meditate, their localized fields sync up together and create an even larger, exponentially more powerful field of coherence that can influence the collective field of consciousness. In this way group meditation can have a powerful effect on large groups of people. Imagine for a moment that you are standing on the dock of a lake. The weather is warm, the water is still, calm, and inviting, and you're in your bathing suit all ready to cool off. You take a running start, launch yourself off the dock, and curl up into a perfect cannonball. You splash down into the water, creating a shockwave of ripples that spread out across the calm lake.

Now, imagine that same dock, but this time you're there with two of your best friends. You link arms, get your running start, and leap off the dock simultaneously. All three of you splash into the water at once creating an even larger shockwave than before, perhaps continuing to the other side of the lake. This is the potential of group meditation, a shockwave of peace and coherence that spreads out through the entire field of consciousness.

This concept is known as the *Maharishi Effect* and in experiments performed by the TM Organization it has been repeatedly demonstrated that large groups of meditators have an effect on the surrounding community. Group meditation creates ripples in the local field, sending out waves of peace and harmony, influencing not only the meditators themselves, but also members of the nearby extended community. These experiments and the theory behind them have been rigorously documented by the TM Organization and in books such as *Permanent Peace* by Robert M. Oates,[1] and *Victory Before War* by Robert Keith Wallace PhD and Jay B. Marcus.[2] This research explains the effects of group meditation to measurably lower crime rates, suicide rates, reduce the number of automobile accidents, increase confidence, optimism, and economic prosperity, improve overall health, and reduce the number of hospital admissions. According to the theory behind the Maharishi Effect, when the square root of 1 percent of a given population is practicing a specific TM technique, a phase coherence, or tipping point is reached, resulting in increased social, political, and economic markers for that community.

Think for a moment of the incredible potential this notion has to literally transform the world we live in. Imagine being able to generate a field of peaceful coherence so powerful that it could eliminate war, terrorism, hostility, and violence of all kinds. Think about how amazing it would be for families, businesses, communities, and nations, to be anchored in a state of personal and social coherence. It would undoubtedly create a world of caring, peace, compassion, kindness, and cooperation. The great yogi sage Patanjali reminds us, "When we are firmly established in nonviolence, all beings around us cease to feel hostility." This nonviolence isn't mood-making or wishing to be more peaceful when we are hiding angry or hostile thoughts within. This is *being peace* from the deepest layer of our being. This is the power of both personal and social coherence to change the world.

I've shared this information with you (which you may find radical, far out, or too crazy to believe) not necessarily to convince you to believe something you don't (see next section), but because in addition to wanting you to have a working understanding of the theory and practice of meditation, I also want the same thing that every beauty pageant contestant has wanted throughout history: world peace! We have an incredible potential to be peacemakers. And now, with meditation in our tool belt, we have perhaps the most powerful means to bring peace to ourselves and the world. If you were to ask me what I believe the cause of violence in the world is, my answer would unquestionably be *stress*. Stress is the emotion of fear, anger, hostility, and rage. These states lead to disharmony and incoherence. They are toxic states for us as individuals and for the greater collective consciousness. Meditation dissolves stress allowing us to let go of fear, release our anger, and transcend the fog of war brought on by hostility and rage. In the stillness of meditation, we not only have the direct experience of peace, but we embody it; we *are* peace. We no longer have to try to be peaceful; it is our essential state of being. This experience creates what I like to call *zenfluence*:

> ˈzen -ˌflü-ən(t)s
>
> noun
> 1. The capacity to bring about a feeling of calm, centeredness, peace, and profound tranquility
> 2. The ability to raise the level of consciousness in an environment by one's presence alone

In my meditation, yoga, and martial arts training, I have experienced individuals who seem to have this unique ability. Perhaps you've also been in the presence of another that somehow, without any effort, exudes a powerful stillness upon the space they occupy. This isn't a quality or power you can wield or fake, nor is it something that can be empirically measured (at least not with our current level of technology). But it can be felt, and deep down, you know there is something different about this person. You, too, have the latent ability to help shift the world's collective consciousness toward the positive. With each meditation, you infuse yourself with more of the attributes of pure spirit, eventually reaching such a critical mass of awareness that it begins to shine forth in all you do.

THE SPIRITUAL BENEFITS OF MEDITATION

> *Personal transformation can and does have global effects. As we go, so goes the world, for the world is us. The revolution that will save the world is ultimately a personal one.*
> —Marianne Williamson

In the end, if you want to help yourself, meditate. If you want to help the world, meditate. It is at the same time the most selfish and the most selfless thing you can do with your life. By being a balanced, genuine, and conscious person, you become a powerful catalyst who brings healing, happiness, and transformation into the world.

THE SCIENCE OF SPIRITUALITY

When discussing the ideas we've been exploring in this chapter with new meditation students, the question invariably arises, "Well, all this conscious universe stuff sounds cool, but how do you know it's true? Can you prove it?" These are exceptionally important questions that perhaps you've had as well. I reply to the question of "Can you prove it?" with, "No, but *you* can."

Several times throughout this book I have referred to the spiritual philosophy of Vedanta, which is one of the world's most ancient and comprehensive wisdom traditions. In Sanskrit, *veda* means "knowledge" and *anta* means "the end of," so Vedanta is the end, the conclusion, the most profound teachings of self-realization. The source of these teachings is an oral tradition going back to remote antiquity, 4,000–6,000 years ago when sages in higher states of consciousness "cognized" universal profound truths and insights. In other words, this knowledge was perceived, realized, or "seen" as if by direct download from the universal soul. These sages don't take credit for these teachings as they have always existed and have been available to the sincere seekers of unity and truth throughout all time. The teachings of Vedanta are not something you believe in, read about, or merely understand intellectually; rather, they are teachings you *experience*. They are not about belief, they are about *knowing*.

Another name for Vedanta is the *science of spirituality*. For many of us, the notion of a "science" of spirituality seems paradoxical or contradictory if not flat-out absurd. Largely thanks to the seventeenth-century philosopher, René Descartes, we live in a dualistic world that divides mind and body, science, and spirit into totally different domains that would appear to make them mutually exclusive. However, Vedanta's beauty lies in its methodology—a systematic approach to exploring the nature of reality in much the same way modern science explores the material universe. Free of beliefs, ideology, dogma, or other religious trappings, Vedanta is a means to discover the truth of existence firsthand. Let's take a closer look at the similarities between the scientific method and how it applies to the Vedantic worldview.

The scientific method followed to this day owes much of its existence to the British scientific philosopher Francis Bacon. His approach of inductive reasoning was instrumental in formulating one of the most effective and reliable means we have for understanding the world. However, the word "scientific" is often co-opted as a means to define something as absolutely valid, proven, legitimate, or true regardless whether or not it actually is (i.e., "scientific" diets, exercise programs, or infomercial products). To define something scientific essentially means that it uses *a systematic and methodical approach to hypothesis and reality testing that leads to reproducible results.*

Five general steps make up the foundation of all forms of scientific research known as the scientific method:

1. **Observe** an aspect or phenomena of the universe.
2. Based upon gathered information, **form a hypothesis** (an educated, calculated prediction) about what is taking place.
3. **Test the hypothesis** for validity through experimentation.

4. Accurately **note and record** your findings to determine if they support or refute the hypothesis.
5. Draw preliminary conclusions, **share or publish your results, and ask your peers (or fellow scientists) to test your hypothesis** by replicating your experiment.

If your conclusions agree with those of your peers (and after multiple similar experiments), then the hypothesis or theory would be considered scientifically valid. This doesn't necessarily mean it's absolutely proven but, in general, it's taken as a strong indication that there's enough evidence to support the conclusion. Now, on the other hand, if your peers *cannot* reproduce your results, the hypothesis is considered questionable if not flat-out wrong and, therefore, an inaccurate description of how the universe behaves. If this happens, the scientist goes back to the drawing board to determine if the error was due to the observation, experimental protocol, or the hypothesis itself. He or she may need to form an entirely new hypothesis to explain what's taking place. This leads to another round of experiments until a consensus is reached by the scientific community. Therefore, the scientific method is a self-correcting and unprejudiced mechanism for weeding out errors, biases, and faulty assumptions to arrive at the *truth*.

You might be thinking, "That's all well and good, but science is about the measurement and repeatable observation of the *objective* universe. Spirituality and meditation are in the realm of subjective experiences and they don't have any objective validity." Philosophers, mystics, and geniuses have all debated this issue for thousands of years. Regardless, that doesn't mean we shouldn't use the same scientific mindset and scrutiny when exploring our inner world. More crucially, the key point often overlooked is this: all our scientific understanding of the universe, from physics to chemistry to geology to biology, can only be known through our *subjective experiences*, or through our *consciousness*. In other words, *science takes place in consciousness*. Therefore, if we truly wish to understand the world, our consciousness and subjective experience are a vital part of the experiment. In the end, it may well turn out that consciousness is all there is.

So, now let's see how these steps correspond to the approach of Vedanta.

To begin with the *observation*, Vedanta notes that there seems to be a more profound, mysterious level of reality that exists beyond the level of our normal perceptions. Past the five senses, we feel a connection—an intuition of something deeper that appears to connect our inner world of thoughts, emotions, and perceptions to the external environment of time, space, material objects, or cause and effect. Or, as Morpheus explains to Neo in *The Matrix*,

"What you know you can't explain, but you feel it. You've felt it your entire life, that there's something wrong with the world. You don't know what it is, but it's there, like a splinter in your mind, driving you mad."

Whether we're actually "driven mad" is a subjective interpretation. However, the point is that it feels as if there's a secret, something hiding behind the scenes of everyday reality coaxing us to look behind the curtain.

Next Vedanta proposes the following *hypothesis*: the separation you feel from the rest of the world is an illusion, an artifact, or mistake of the intellect. The true nature of reality is unity, oneness, pure spirit; the immeasurable potential for all that exists, for all that was, and for all that will be. This reality is without beginning or ending, without birth or death. It is the core of all beings, the source of all that exists.

Vedanta also explains that the everyday world we engage in is a projection from this deeper level of consciousness and our experiences of it come to us in one of four different ways: feeling, thought, action, or being. Your true nature is pure spirit and the purpose of life is to restore the memory of your true identity.

THE SPIRITUAL BENEFITS OF MEDITATION 137

Vedanta goes on to lay out the following testing methodology to validate the hypothesis of one reality. For each of the four modes of experience there exists a corresponding vehicle through which we can return to our true nature. These four approaches are known as *yogas* or paths back to union. They are as follows:

1. *Bhakti Yoga*: The path of feeling. This is the path of love in all its expressions; love of self, love of others, love of the divine or God. This yoga embodies the relationship of our individual soul to the universal spirit in all the forms it takes.
2. *Gyana Yoga*: The path of thinking. This is the yoga of the mind, the intellect, reason, science and discovery. The path of using the mind to go beyond the mind.
3. *Karma Yoga*: The path of action. This is the yoga of service to others without the need for reward or ego gratification. It is the performance of action and duty in service to the divine in all beings.
4. *Raja Yoga*: The path of being. This is the yoga of meditation and all its allied disciplines. It is discovering the truth at the heart of reality through direct experience.

As a practical and experiential spiritual philosophy, Vedanta doesn't demand that you simply accept or believe in its hypothesis; rather, it identifies these four paths as the routes to self-realization and enlightenment, and encourages you to test them in the laboratory of your life. It says: Here are the paths back to unity, follow the one that's appropriate for you, run the experiment, and see what happens.

Now, as we practice one of the four yogas, we can *note and record our experiences*. For example, using our lives as the testing environment:

- Assess and measure the stages of growth in our personal and subjective experience. Take note of the changes you experience in body, mind, insights, perceptions, creativity, and shifts in

awareness. Identify these as an indication that a transformation is taking place.
- Recognize a lessening of emotional- or ego-based reactivity as a signal that you are becoming increasingly comfortable with the mystery and uncertainty of life.
- Be vigilant for hints that the gaps between our outer and inner worlds are shrinking. Notice and record sensations of timelessness, unity, or non-locality.
- Write down instances that indicate your spiritual journey is deepening—increasing lightheartedness, happiness, joy, and bliss; an intimate sense of connection to all of life; or the acceleration of coincidence and synchronicities that guide you toward the fulfillment of your desires.
- Become aware of changes in the type or quality of your relationships. As you grow and evolve, the type or number of relationships you have may change as you are drawn to different pockets of collective consciousness.
- Notice shifts in the qualities and traits making up your personality transform from ego to spirit. Become aware of instances when you choose to minimize your own self-importance in order to help and serve others while remaining deeply established in peace, harmony, laughter, and love.
- Track the evolution of your desires from personal, material-based wants and needs to more universal intentions of happiness, healing, and compassion for others.
- Take note of the increasing instances in which your ground state is deeply established in peace, harmony, laughter, and love.

This is by no means a complete list. Countless additional clues of your progress will show up as you travel your personal path back to union. The key is to be aware, curious, and open to the transformation that's taking place within. Since the changes may often be subtle or something you consider trivial, keeping a journal can be especially helpful in measuring your progress. In hindsight something you thought was meaningless might have been an indication from the universe that something amazing was happening. Recording your experience is powerful way in which we can document that real transformation is taking place, rather than thinking it's all in our imagination.

Finally, having run your experiment, you are equipped to *draw your conclusions*. Is the hypothesis of one reality valid? Does your evidence and experience support the hypothesis? If so, deep down, you will know that it's true. You can share your experiences and findings with peers of like-minded seekers of union through writing or teaching in ways that encourage others to run their own experiment.

On the other hand, if your experiences do not produce the results that agree with the one reality as described in the Vedic literature, you are under no obligation to believe it. If the hypothesis doesn't suit you or provide evidence to support it, it should be rejected. Don't take anything on belief or faith alone. A worldview, ideology, or philosophy should only be adopted if it agrees with your direct experience and common sense.

Or as the Buddha reminds us:

> *Do not believe in what you have heard.*
> *Do not believe in tradition because it is*
>   *handed down many generations.*
> *Do not believe in anything that has been spoken many times.*
> *Do not believe because the written statements*
>   *come from some old sage.*
> *Do not believe in conjecture.*
> *Do not believe in authority or teachers or elders.*
> *But after careful observation and analysis, when*
>   *it agrees with reason and it will benefit one*
>   *and all, then accept it and live by it.*

Distilling this wisdom down even more concisely, in perhaps his most quoted aphorism, Bruce Lee states: "Absorb what is useful, discard what is useless and add what is specifically your own."

This scientific, experiential approach to exploring our reality is what sets Vedanta apart from other spiritual philosophies or religions. It observes the universe we live in, states the hypothesis of unity, and encourages us to each test the theory by following one of the four yogic paths. It is a self-reliant approach to explore and discover the truth personally and directly. It is a path well-trodden by countless seekers throughout time and space who have pierced the veil of illusion on the journey back to oneness.

THE ROYAL PATH

As meditators, we are all raja yogis. Raja means "king" and raja yoga is known as the "royal path to union." Like a plentiful and flourishing kingdom, its study provides us with the riches of knowledge, experience, and expanded awareness. It is king of all the paths to union; however, it is not exclusive. As I mentioned earlier, *anyone can meditate*. With discipline and practice we can all benefit by practicing raja yoga.

Raja yoga focuses on practices and techniques that shift our awareness within and help us to experience the underlying unity of our mind, body, and spirit. The most detailed explanation of raja yoga comes to us through the *Yoga Sutras of Patanjali*. Written over 1,700 years ago, these 196 sutras or aphorisms describe the eight branches or limbs of raja yoga practice, giving us a detailed route to follow on our path back to union.

The eight limbs of raja yoga, or *ashtanga*, as detailed in *The Seven Spiritual Laws of Yoga* are as follows:[3]

1. Yama: The rules of social behavior or the spontaneous evolutionary behavior of conscious beings. These rules are guidelines for our behavior when interacting with others. But rather than

viewing the yamas as hard-and-fast rules of conduct, instead think of them as the most appropriate and life-affirming choices available to us in our daily encounters with others. The five yamas are:

- *Ahimsa* or nonviolence
- *Satya* or truthfulness
- *Brahmacharya* or appropriate use of sexual and creative energy
- *Asteya* or honesty
- *Aparigraha* or generosity

2. Niyama: The rules of personal behavior or the internal dialogue of conscious beings. Whereas the yamas are guidelines for interacting with others, you can think of the niyamas as the way we act and think when no one is watching. The five niyamas are:

- *Saucha* or purity
- *Santosha* or contentment
- *Tapas* or discipline
- *Svadhyana* or self-study
- *Ishwara pranidhana* or surrender to the divine

3. Asana: Physical postures or mind-body integration. This is what most people think of when they hear the word yoga. Asana means "seat" or "position" and refers to both movements and static poses that cultivate flexibility, strength, balance, and unified mind, body, and spirit. While this branch has become the most visible and popular component of yoga in the West, it's important to note that the original purpose for asana was primarily to create and maintain a healthy, strong, and flexible body so one could sit in meditation for extended periods of time.

4. Pranayama: Breath control or mastery of the internal life force. "Prana" means vital life essence and pranayama is the management of that life force through breathing. Different breathing exercises cultivate a deep state of neurorespiratory integration and influence the entire mind-body system. Pranayama techniques

can energize, calm, or steady the body and mind, thereby creating a more ideal atmosphere for meditation practice.

5. Pratyahara: Control of the senses or tuning into our subtle sensory experiences. Pratyahara can be thought of as a form of sensory fasting in which we pull our attention inward and away from the external world. When we regularly take time away from the world for a little while and let our senses rest, we find our experiences to be more vibrant. Pratyahara is also about paying attention to the sensory impressions we experience each day so to minimize toxic influences and maximize those that are nourishing for our mind and body. Pratyahara occurs naturally whenever we close our eyes to meditate in a quiet and settled environment.

6. Dharana: Control of the mind and mastery of intention and attention. Remembering that reality is a selective act of attention and interpretation, Dharana encourages us to be aware that what we put our attention on will grow stronger in our lives and what we withdraw attention from will fade away. Attention is our greatest personal resource and what we do with it matters. While attention energizes, intention is the transformative power that can bring about powerful changes in our lives. Recognizing the power of intentions and become aware of them in our lives can more easily lead to their fulfillment.

7. Dhyana: Meditation and cultivating witnessing awareness. The practice of meditation cultivates the experience of "space" in which we can observe our mental activity without reacting to it. Dhyana is the state of non-change amid the turbulent activity of our minds. We are the witness of our thoughts and can be engaged in the world but not overshadowed by its drama.

8. Samadhi: Being completely absorbed in pure spirit. This is the experience of infinite, immortal, timeless awareness. In samadhi, we merge into our true essence. Unified with the field of potential

of all that has been, all that is, and all that ever will be. We know our true selves to be that of eternal, non-local awareness playing a unique role on the stage of human evolution.

The practice of meditation, along with the eight limbs of yoga previously described, form the methodology for the experiment of self-exploration that helps us discover our true identity. Ultimately, that's what meditation's true purpose is. All the physical, mental, and emotional aspects of the practice are wonderful added benefits, but when all is said and done mediation is a means to pull back the mask and see who we really are—a soul, a wave on the ocean of spirit expressing itself for a brief moment in time on the shores of the cosmic ocean.

Your experiment awaits.

CHAPTER 7

PERFORMANCE BENEFITS

Before we conclude our exploration of the numerous benefits meditation has to offer, there's one additional category I'd like to examine. These are the benefits related specifically to performance, leadership, and the business world. With the expanding acceptance of meditation and mindfulness in Western culture, an ever-growing number of corporate executives, military and political leaders, athletes, and other peak performers are embracing meditation and singing its praises. But what is it that makes meditation so attractive to these individuals? As we've already discovered in the previous chapters, there are dozens of physical, mental, emotional, and spiritual reasons to practice meditation. These highly successful and driven individuals, however, espouse and practice meditation for two additional reasons: 1) it improves performance and 2) it's good for business.

Here are a just a few of the big-name companies that have begun to integrate meditation and mindfulness practice into their corporate culture:

- General Mills
- Apple
- Google
- Nike
- AOL Time Warner
- Yahoo!

- Proctor & Gamble
- HBO
- Intel
- Aetna

These business giants have caught on to the fact that meditation is more than a fad or trend; *it's an evidence-based approach to directly impact performance and productivity at every level of an organization.*

But what specifically does meditation bring to the office, boardroom, conference table, and playing field? In looking at some of the results both large and small businesses have experienced upon embracing a corporate meditation or mindfulness-based approach, a familiar pattern of attributes begins to appear—and interestingly, these are the same qualities that define a successful business.

- Structure, stability, and centeredness: A secure foundation, strong mission, and clear vision
- Relationships: A network of like-minded individuals and thought partners who share a common vision
- Innovation and creativity: The ability to produce new and original ideas
- Adaptability: Being able to flow and grow with the changing economic climate, technological evolution, and the demands and needs of the consumer
- Resilience: The ability to cope with stress and adversity and bounce back from negative experiences
- Emotional intelligence: The capacity to be aware of, control, and express one's emotions, and to handle interpersonal relationships judiciously and empathetically
- Ethical leadership: Leadership driven by values, responsibility, transparency, and sustainability
- Compassion: Concern for others; the motivation to relieve another's suffering

- Service/social responsibility mentality: Acting from a place of caring, empathy, compassion, and service to one's clients or customers

Without these qualities, it's unlikely that a business will be able to succeed and last over time, or that the employees will want to continue to work there. If present, however, these elements can spell long-term success for a company, business, or even an entire country. They are the foundational pillars of success that allow companies to grow and thrive in an environment of perpetual change.

Let's explore the influence of meditation on each of these key attributes in some detail.

MEDITATION FOSTERS STABILITY

When we practice meditation, we feel safe, solid, and centered. It helps to ground us in the present moment so we feel less swept about by the ever-changing circumstances of our lives. People often refer to the practice of meditation as the act of *coming home to ourselves*. In that sense of "home" we feel stable and clear, a quality that begins to become a part of us, no matter what external situations arise. It builds a sense of silent power, a strength that shields us from anything that might disturb our peace of mind.

In a business or high-performance environment, having this sense of stability and groundedness is an enormous asset. Corporations and businesses are often in a state of flux as they adapt to the changing times and needs of their customers or shareholders. Organizational restructuring or rebranding can leave employees feeling out of control and uncertain about the future. This can naturally lead to feelings of stress and anxiety which, for reasons already discussed can impact performance, absenteeism, work-life balance, and a sense of job fulfillment. Under these conditions, meditation helps to manage the stress of uncertainty and helps us to feel anchored in the stillness we carry within us. Like a mountain, we can remain stable and rooted as the winds of change blow around us.

MEDITATION ENHANCES RELATIONSHIPS

The practice of meditation helps to establish a greater connection with others. As old (and sometimes defensive) conditioning falls away, we feel our boundaries soften and we are able to more easily identify with the needs of others. We become more attuned to our families, friends, and coworkers and have increasing insight into what makes others tick. This isn't some form of mystical psychobabble but rather, after having gained insight into our own lives through our practice, we can apply that knowledge to others and see the feelings and experiences we share with all of humanity. We see others as our mirror and a deeper bond can form between us. It fosters the spirit of "being in this together" with everyone we interact with. In this state, conflicts decrease, connections are forged, and communication can take place from a much deeper level.

The corporate world, whether it is willing to admit it or not, is built around relationships. Indeed, relationships are the fabric that holds businesses together. The health of a company is directly related to its relationships with clients, customers, shareholders, teammates, leaders, and executives. Through the practice of meditation, we enhance our professional and personal relationships in these key ways:

1. We become better listeners. By spending regular time in stillness, we create space to hear the concerns and needs of others. With our egos taking a back seat, we can put more of our attention on what others have to say. More often than not, we listen not with the intention to understand, but with the intention to reply. Meditation presses the mute button on our self-interest channel so we can be more attentive to others.

2. We speak more skillfully. Consistent meditation quiets our inner dialogue so that when we speak our words are more intentional and have greater clarity of purpose. Our speech takes on the quality of impeccability, meaning that we refrain from saying anything that could be considered cruel or hurtful. This is the embodiment of this potent quote by Sai Baba: "Before you speak, ask yourself, is it kind, is it necessary, is it true, does it improve on the silence?"
3. We become more sensitive to how we can help meet the needs of others in the workplace. Without our internal dialogue barking in our minds so loudly, we are more attuned to other's energy. I don't necessarily mean some kind of new-agey hocus-pocus here; I'm simply referring to being able to read or intuit what's going on with others. Whether it's through body language, the tone of their voice, the look in their eyes, other non-verbal cues, or just a gut feeling you have, as your meditation practice deepens, you may find yourself developing a greater insight into other's feelings. This can be a great way to "read" someone so you know the best time to discuss an important project, provide feedback, or ask for some vacation time.
4. We become less judgmental. With meditation comes compassion and as compassion grows, the need to be judgmental begins to wane. As discussed in Chapter 3, compassion cultivates a recognition that in many ways, everyone we meet is *just like me*. It's easy to judge another when we think they are vastly different than us. However, when the gap between us and them, or me and the other, begins to get blurry through meditation practice, judging another becomes more difficult. We start to understand that while we may not agree with something they may have said or done, if all things had been equal and we had been in a similar situation, we might have made the same choice. This can be a great revelation for us and it helps us to create a mind that is

a judgment-free zone. In this space, our relationships become more nurturing and productive.

MEDITATION CULTIVATES CREATIVITY AND INNOVATION

As we briefly touched on in Chapter 5, the stillness of meditation is the fertile field from which new ideas and concepts arise. Contrary to popular belief, creativity is not the result of brainstorming or thinking long and hard about a problem. While those components might be involved, the emergence of a new and creative idea is a spontaneous event rooted deep in the settled field of infinite possibilities. Creativity, like meditation, can't be forced; however, it can be cultivated, and meditation plays in critical role in its development.

CREATIVITY DECONSTRUCTED

Creativity isn't a single act; it's a process by which something new and unexpected unfolds from the mind of the universe. The steps of this process, as taught by Deepak Chopra, are as follows.[1]

1. **Clarity of the intended outcome**: All new ideas begin with the image of a specific result in mind. What is the intended end product? A strong healthy body, a book, a new business, a skyscraper, or an attraction at a theme park? All manifestation begins with an intention. Once the intention is well defined (the what), the mechanisms for its fulfillment (the how's) will begin to arrange themselves.
2. **Information gathering**: Great creators and inventors immerse themselves in resources related to what they wish to manifest. They become subject-matter experts on their topic, exploring every angle and perspective, learning everything they can as it relates to the field.

3. **Information reshuffling**: Once the new information has been collected and absorbed, it will then go through a process of re-organization, recombining, editing, and rearranging. Data, ideas, and concepts, like puzzle pieces on a table, will get repositioned as new patterns begin to form.
4. **Incubation**: With the first three steps complete, now it's time to take a step back, detach, and allow the auto-correlation and infinite organizing power of the universal mind to take over. To quote one of the greatest creative minds humanity has ever known, Leonardo da Vinci: "Every now and then go away, have a little relaxation, for when you come back to your work your judgment will be surer. Go some distance away because then the work appears smaller and more of it can be taken in at a glance and a lack of harmony and proportion is more readily seen."

    Incubation is the stage of the creative process in which we unleash the power of meditation. As we unplug from our intellect and thinking mind, we literally enter the realm of unbounded creativity and infinite imagination. By surrendering into the sea of pure awareness we open the gateway by which the creative response will express itself through us. This step of incubation and meditation is critical, for without the period of stillness and gestation we will stay trapped at the level of the mind and intellect rather than diving deeper into the fertile field of unlimited possibilities.
5. **Insight**: When the time is right, the probability wave will collapse into a singularity and insight will "pop" into conscious awareness. The creative response will produce the "aha" moment in which a new idea explodes into existence.
6. **Inspiration**: With the spike of insight comes the emotional thrill of inspiration. The word inspiration comes from the Latin *inspirare*, which means "to breathe or blow into," so it should come with little surprise that we feel inspired we often take a sudden

gasp of air. This feeling is the flood of spirit, joy, enthusiasm, and energy that accompanies the new idea or thought. Deep within we recognize that this creation is something that is totally new and has never been before.

7. **Implementation and integration**: Finally, the new idea is ready to be made tangible in the world. It can be implemented, mapped out, blueprinted, process-flowed, and ultimately ushered into existence.

MEDITATION PROMOTES ADAPTABILITY

As we previously discussed, meditation helps to open up access to a more unconditioned mental state. From this more boundless perspective, it becomes easier to relinquish the need to cling to old beliefs, habits of thought, and preconceived notions. In other words, we become more flexible, more open to change, new ideas, and different approaches. When we rigidly hang on to the past or "how we've always done it" we lock ourselves out from the current of evolution that is flowing through all of life. Meditative awareness dissolves this rigidity so we can be pliable and adaptive in all situations.

> *You must be shapeless, formless, like water. When you pour water in a cup, it becomes the cup. When you pour water in a bottle, it becomes the bottle. When you pour water in a teapot, it becomes the teapot. Water can drip and it can crash. Become like water my friend.*
>
> —Bruce Lee

MEDITATION ENHANCE RESILIENCE

In the spaciousness and "observer awareness" brought on through meditation we begin to see the world and ourselves with more objectivity. We take things less personally and, in doing so, we're less emotionally attached, triggered, and reactive. With time, our tendency to over-react decreases and we're more able to bounce back from stress and let go of perceived slights, insults, or negativity. We recover more quickly from difficulties or challenges and are able to see through the melodrama and hysteria of life that seems to hold our society in its grasp.

In this regard, meditation is the ultimate *adaptogen*. This term comes from herbal medicine and refers to a natural substance that helps the body adapt to stress, to normalize bodily processes, and return its systems to a state of homeostasis or balance. In light of all the physiological and mental benefits to meditation we've already explored, meditation seems to fit that definition to the letter. Meditation returns the mind and body to a state of balance from which we are much more likely to recover quickly and easily from changes or stresses in the office, boardroom, or playing field.

I'd like to pause here and tell you how my practice of meditation helped build resilience at one period in my life.

From 1997 through 2002, I was a resort hotel bellman and valet. I was one of a staff of about twenty people who personally assisted hotel guests by greeting them, unloading luggage from their car, parking it securely in the parking lot, storing luggage, escorting the guests and delivering their luggage to their room, and answering any and all manner of questions about the hotel (all of these steps would also be performed in reverse when we checked the guest out of the hotel at the end of their stay).

At this hotel, the bell staff didn't earn a normal hourly wage, or even minimum wage for that matter. We made what was called "tip-time," which amounted to $3.25 per hour, *plus gratuities*. So essentially, we worked almost entirely for the tips we made from our guest interactions. The majority of the time the guests would tip us for our service (usually about $3.00–$5.00 for parking or retrieving a vehicle or storing luggage and $2.00 per bag for checking in or out of the room). However, there were times when the guests didn't tip. Not receiving a tip was known as getting stiffed, and it could be a tough pill to swallow. After giving a guest five to twenty minutes of your undivided attention, answering questions, carrying luggage, or running back and forth to the parking lot to park their car, getting stiffed felt lousy. First, you feel rejected and invalidated. Second, since you make your living from the tips you get, anxiety about having enough money starts to creep in on top of the rejection. To add insult to injury, some guests wouldn't even say thank you, let alone give you a tip.

Furthermore, in this hotel, the bell staff didn't pool their tips together; it was everyone for themselves, so to speak. However, it wasn't a free for all; we all couldn't just jump on the next arriving guest; we had a rotation system so each bellman or valet had to wait their turn in line to help the next guest. So imagine this scenario: you've just arrived at work on a Sunday morning (big checkout day), you get in rotation, and wait for your first chance to help a guest. When you get your guest, bad news—you get stiffed. Back in line for five to fifteen minutes. Second guest, stiffed again. Back to rotation. Third guest, stiff. Fourth guest, stiff. Fifth guest, you guessed it—stiffed. (As hard to imagine as it sounds, this would happen.)

By this point, you've pretty much had it. Many of us after such a string of strikeouts would either get depressed and despondent, or outright angry, shaking our fists at the sky yelling "Why God . . . WHY?"

Now I can't speak for all bellmen and valets, but the crew I worked with were pretty superstitious folks and when they couldn't handle facing another round of "bellman roulette" they would often ask the bell captain to take them out of line, believing that they were in a "bad rotation"—that their place in the lineup had been cursed by the bell services gods and sitting it out in the break room for a few minutes would cause their luck to magically change. If this didn't work, many—so overwhelmed by rejection—would seek out the manager on duty and ask to go home for the day.

Where am I going with this you might ask? Well, it was around this same time (1997) that I learned to meditate. And it was in this environment I got to experience firsthand the power of meditation to help foster a more resilient mental environment. As we've already discussed, one of meditation's many benefits is the ability to take life less seriously and less personally. With my continuing practice, I became increasingly able to detach from the outcome of my guest interaction and focus more on doing my job in the present moment. I could just perform my duty (karma yoga) without getting worried or anxious if I got stiffed. I could have the intention to do my best, step into the uncertainty, and let the universe handle the results.

Does that mean I always got tipped? No. And it still didn't feel terrific when I got stiffed, but rather reacting from a place of anger or indignation, I was able to face it with a shrug and move on, thereby minimizing the negative charge generated by an emotional outburst. Meditation also opened up the space for me to see that any negative reaction I had from a situation only polluted my consciousness, which would subtly cascade into my next guest interaction, influencing how it would play out. I could bounce back and not let the situation infect the rest of my day.

This is the real-world power of meditation to build resilience in the face of adversity. Life isn't always easy, but with the mental flexibility and space created through regular practice, we become able to reinterpret our reality in ways that enhance both our growth and happiness.

MEDITATION STRENGTHENS EMOTIONAL INTELLIGENCE

Maturely and skillfully managing emotions is a foundational ability that is considered by many experts to be more important than overall knowledge or aptitude in a given field. In the most basic sense, we can distill emotional intelligence down to the understanding that success in life and business is less about what happens to us and more about *how we respond* to what happens to us.

> *Attitude is more important than facts. It is more important than the past, than education, money, circumstances, than failures and success, than what other people think, say, or do. It is more important than appearance, ability, or skill. It will make or break a business, a home, a friendship, an organization. The remarkable thing is I have a choice every day of what my attitude will be. I cannot change my past. I cannot change the actions of others. I cannot change the inevitable. The only thing I can change is attitude. Life is ten percent what happens to me and ninety percent how I react to it.*
>
> —Charles R. Swindoll

Meditation can play a pivotal role in developing emotional intelligence. The regular experience of stillness and silence helps to open a door to self-reflection from which several key benefits arise.

- Overall lower levels of stress and anxiety: In today's fast-paced, performance-based work environment, calm is a superpower that cannot be overstated. Remaining grounded and centered allows us to perceive and think clearly, to communicate mindfully, and to act decisively.
- Awareness of, rather than reaction to, thoughts and emotions: The more we practice witnessing our mental and emotional landscape

without interpretation or judgment, the more detached we can be when dealing with the ups and downs of our day-to-day emotions. Challenging situations still occur, but by witnessing instead of participating in them, we lessen the emotional charge, allowing us to skillfully navigate our way through the storm.

- Transcend habitual emotional conditioning: Our emotional responses and control dramas are often formed early in life and become habitual patterns through repeated practice. In the pause or space of witnessing awareness, we can bypass our programming long enough to weigh the consequences of inappropriate or unproductive emotional states and replace them with more supportive and nourishing ones.
- Understanding the emotional needs of others: As we gain insight into our emotions, we become more understanding of the feelings of others. Our skill in managing our own emotions helps us better relate to family members, peers, clients, and customers. We can more easily read their emotional energy, anticipate how to best interact, and meet their needs.
- Down-regulate the ego: Family or work conflicts are often rooted in a sense separation at the level of the ego. Competing needs for validation, acceptance, recognition, and approval often results in personality clashes that can strain relationships. Meditation, however, helps to dissolve the separateness of the ego boundary, allowing us to bond more easily with coworkers or family. We more easily recognize that we are each part of a whole that works together coherently for a common goal, rather than as individual egos competing for supremacy.

MEDITATION CULTIVATES ETHICAL LEADERSHIP

Tapping into our soul through regular meditation brings about an evolution in consciousness, the byproduct of which is the development of key character traits that promote ethical beliefs and values. Similar to the yamas and niyamas of *Patanjali's Yoga Sutras* discussed in Chapter 6, these qualities aren't as much rules to be self-imposed as they are the spontaneous behaviors of individuals and leaders established in unity consciousness:

- Honesty
- Trust
- Integrity
- Respect
- Responsibility
- Humility
- Fidelity
- Fairness
- Compassion
- Selflessness

This isn't meant to be a complete list; it is, however, a good representation of the core values strengthened through a regular meditation practice. The more time we spend in the stillness of unbounded awareness, the more our being is infused with the attributes of pure spirit—calling us to lead from the level of our soul.

It's important to note that these qualities aren't mood-making or tactics that we "try to become." We don't have to strive to be honest, responsible, fair, or humble. Instead, these traits arise organically and effortlessly and, eventually, they replace more self-serving attitudes and ego-driven needs. It becomes easier to recognize that the needs of the many outweigh the wants of the few. Our leadership, therefore, rather than being a set of rules or an extension of our personality, becomes a reflection of our *higher self.*

MEDITATION FOSTERS COMPASSION

We've discussed the relationship between meditation and compassion several times in this book, so I won't rehash those details here. However, I think it's important to consider the value of cultivating compassion in business or other performance-related fields. In the professional world, it's often an expectation (either spoken or unspoken) to beat the competition, outperform the previous year's profits, ambitiously drive toward future goals, and perhaps sacrifice the balance and wellness of ourselves and our coworkers in the name of ongoing success. Compassion, by comparison seems like a "soft" mentality, perhaps even a weakness when viewed through the lens of professional or corporate gain. However, as we are reminded by His Holiness the Dalai Lama, "Compassion and tolerance are not a sign of weakness, but a sign of strength." It is the reminder that, ultimately, we're all on this journey together; when we genuinely care about each other—even our competitors—it transforms not only us as individuals, but our teams, our departments, and our entire corporate culture.

When compassion is lacking, we feel unappreciated, disengaged, and uncared for. This ultimately leads to suffering in the workplace and an overall lack of enthusiasm for our jobs or roles. However, where compassion thrives, there is greater mindfulness toward the needs and feelings of others, sensitivity to communication, collaboration, recognition, and a sense of security in the organization valuing us as individuals, not just as worker bees in a vast, uncaring hive. Compassion leads us to the high ground of evolutionary choices for everyone involved; it fosters concern for all with whom we interact. Compassion elevates businesses, teams, classrooms, and communities. It is the glue that holds together the human family in a web of caring, understanding, and love.

Meditation is the gateway to building and nurturing compassion at all these levels. When we are free from the burden of stress and anxiety, when we can see and think clearly, when we know our true nature, compassion is the natural byproduct. It is who and what we are, and bringing that to the workplace can affect the lives of others in ways we can't imagine.

MEDITATION CREATES A SERVICE-BASED MENTALITY

Through regular meditation, the ego personality is gradually down-regulated, softening its persistent subtext of "What's in it for me," "What do I get out of this," "It's not my problem," or "I've got mine, who cares about anyone else?" The ego is a self-serving mental construct; it usually couldn't care less about anyone or anything outside of itself, and if it does want anything, it's generally seeking another's approval. However, meditation exposes the ego's attention-hungry, self-centered illusions for what they are, and in the light of awareness, those illusions begin to have less and less power over us. Our focus begins to move away from ourselves, we start to see and care about others, and we want to help relieve their suffering.

"What's in it for me?" becomes "How can I help, how can I serve," and "What do you need me to do for you?" Coming from a place of service to others signals a profound shift in our consciousness. The world no longer revolves around us. Yes, we're still a unique focal point, a distinct wave on the ocean of spirit, but now we want to help the other waves to be happy and fulfilled as well.

If you've ever worked in the service industry, you're undoubtedly familiar with the standard greeting of "How can I help you?" used in most stores, restaurants, and hotels. It's an affirmation that we are here to assist others. While some might consider working in the service industry demeaning or below their station in life, it's interesting to note that in some parts of the world working in the service or hospitality industry is a position of great honor and nobility. This is due to a deep cultural affinity with serving others. It is considered a privilege to assist another with their needs.

It is in this regard that meditation can have such a profound effect on our organizations, teams, and businesses. When a service mentality is present, we choose to help and serve, not just because it's part of our job description, but because *we genuinely want to help others*. This isn't an excuse to let ourselves be walked on or taken advantage of. Being someone's doormat doesn't help anyone. However, a service-based mindset is one in which our personal code of behavior comes from the genuine desire to help, whether that's by helping a coworker with a project, volunteering to do a mundane task that no one enjoys, or offering a few encouraging words to someone having a rough day. We do what we do because deep within, we want to make the world a better place.

Now, the ego will sometimes resist and regain its dominance or feign offense for "lowering itself to serve others," but this is just part of its game. Meditation teaches us not to take the world personally. It's not about me, this is just the role I'm playing; it's part of my duty to serve the divine in you and all other sentient beings.

We've previously discussed the path of selfless service known as karma yoga, one of the four paths to liberation and unity consciousness. It is described by many as the most effective means to evolve spiritually. When we practice karma yoga, we give selflessly to others without attachment to the results of our actions. Recognizing another as the embodiment of divine consciousness, we surrender ourselves to the god or goddess in disguise through the act of service.

Whether you call it karma yoga or service-based work doesn't really matter. What's important is that through meditation, this quality is cultivated and it can have a tremendous impact on how businesses, schools, organizations, teams, and families relate to each other. When we recognize that part of our purpose for being here is to support others, we truly step into the flow of life.

These qualities—all sustained and strengthened through the practice of meditation—are what make businesses, schools, teams, and athletes excel. They are routinely displayed in classrooms, playing fields, boardrooms, shareholder meetings, planning consultations, and strategy sessions. They round out the already robust list of benefits meditation has to offer. All that remains for you to take advantage of these benefits is to start your own regular successful meditation practice.

PART 3
BUILDING A PRACTICE

CHAPTER 8

CREATING A SUCCESSFUL MEDITATION PRACTICE

Up until this point, we've been describing all the benefits of a regular meditation practice. Hopefully learning about those benefits has inspired you to make meditation an ongoing part of your life. With all those positive effects of meditation, however, there is one downside: *you have to do it*! In all honesty, I could talk to you all day long about how powerful and impactful meditation is for every layer of your being and how it will transform you from the inside out, but it would be just that—*talking* about it rather than actually *doing* it. And if you want to experience the benefits of meditation, there's no escaping the fact that you just have to do it.

Ultimately, everything we have discussed so far has been preparation for creating your own practice of meditation. The background isn't necessary; however, it has hopefully created the "hook" to get you to commit to a regular practice. Taking a deep dive into the history, theory, and benefits can be interesting and create some emotional leverage for making meditation more than something you just read about, but what we want to look at now is setting ourselves up as successful meditators. The rest is just gravy.

This chapter, therefore, is about giving you the skills to integrate meditation into your life. We're going to cover all the details you need to perfect your practice and make it work for you. You don't need to understand religion, philosophy, or science to be a successful meditator.

All you need to do is pay attention to the following recommendations. If you make use of these practical suggestions, you'll be able to meditate happily for many years to come.

TWO TYPES OF MEDITATORS

Before we dig into the specifics, let's talk about the two types of meditators so you can decide which you would like to be.

First, we have what can be called a *crisis meditator*. A crisis meditator is someone who, as the name suggests, turns to meditation when stress or life circumstances become overwhelming. This is someone who has learned meditation, but only uses it as a contingency measure when they are under extreme stress. For them, meditation is a *reactive* tool that sits tucked away behind a window that says, "Break Glass in Case of Emergency." They typically only turn to meditation when they're going through a rough patch or when life throws them a curve ball.

Let me say this—there's nothing wrong with being a crisis meditator. I'm happy when someone practices meditation—no matter the reason or how frequent the practice. Crisis meditating will work. As we've seen, practicing meditation, even sporadically, will have an effect. It will mitigate the stress response and help us better manage the challenges we all go through on a daily basis.

With that being said, being a crisis meditator is not as effective as the second type of meditator, which we can simply refer to as a *regular meditator*. As you've guessed, regular meditators are people who make meditation a consistent, *proactive*, ongoing practice and part of their lifestyle. For them, meditation has become as natural as tying their shoelaces or brushing their teeth; it's just something they do—every day without fail. It's a habit that feels normal. In fact, for most regular meditators, it probably feels strange or odd when they miss a meditation.

The key difference between these two types of meditators is this: While both meditators will receive benefit from their practice, the regular meditators, over time, begin to retrain their nervous systems to a calmer state in which the emergencies that compel a crisis meditator to practice have a much less upsetting affect. That is to say, because they continue to practice and the benefits continue to accrue, regular meditators find the challenges of life to be less overwhelming.

I often liken crisis or reactive meditators to tourists. They visit a new destination, take in the sights, enjoy the cuisine, and visit with the locals. But ultimately, they're only there for a limited amount of time and can't always get a fuller picture of the destination. A permanent resident, however, is familiar with all the hangouts, knows the best places to visit, the shortest routes, and all the unique flavors of the country. They know the place and call it home.

In the end, it's all about what works for you, but know that if you make meditation practice a consistent part of your daily routine, the tempests of life won't be able to toss you around as much because you'll be carrying the calm eye of the storm with you wherever you go.

With that said, let's explore how to make meditation work for us.

PREPARING TO MEDITATE

Before we begin to meditate, it's helpful to set the stage and prepare ourselves both mentally and physically. First, we want to find the right place to meditate—preferably creating a relatively disturbance-free environment. This can be helpful, especially when we're just starting out. Once you've been meditating for some time, you'll be able to slip into stillness wherever you can sit down and close your eyes. But in the beginning, finding a quiet place to tuck yourself away is like having a fenced-in field to plant the seeds of peace and harmony—it helps support your practice and keeps the interruptions to a minimum. Dim the lights, turn off your cell phone, close the door, and consciously withdraw from the activity of the world for a little while. Since the so-hum meditation is a silent technique, we also refrain from playing music during our meditations. Music, even soft instrumental or calming ambient pieces, have the effect of keeping our attention at the level of the senses and mind, triggering associations or memories. Therefore, unless it's part of a specific guided meditation technique, try to keep your meditation space as quiet as possible.

Although it's not required, having a regular dedicated space for your meditation can be beneficial. It doesn't have to be an entire room; a small corner or alcove with a chair and an end table can work nicely. The benefit of having a consistent location to meditate is that it creates a sense of familiarity for your mind and body, eventually becoming associated with your practice of meditation. Just as different rooms in a house are used for specific activities, your regular meditation space will remind you of its unique purpose each time you sit down to practice. In addition, some individuals find that with continued practice their meditation space begins to embody the qualities of stillness, peace, or holiness. In the same way an ancient cathedral has a feeling of sacred space and powerful spiritual energy, a meditation room or nook can capture and embody the qualities of deep stillness cultivated during the practice.

You may also wish to set up a small altar or shelf that holds icons, archetypes, images, a candle, mala beads, fresh flowers, or a chime. Anything that has personal or spiritual significance may be a helpful way to anchor yourself and focus your intentions before beginning to meditate. It is entirely a matter of personal preference. Feel free to experiment and find what works best for you.

Candles and incense can also be useful in creating the desired environment for meditation. By burning a scented candle or your favorite stick of incense prior to meditation, you can create a state of neuro-associative conditioning in which you begin to link the aroma with the relaxation of meditation. Eventually, just the smell alone can create a deeply relaxing response in your mind and body. One word of caution, some candles and incense can have powerful fragrances that, if kept burning in a confined space, may become overwhelming and interrupt your practice. You don't want to have to stop halfway through your meditation to air out the room. I recommend lightly "dusting" a space with a scent briefly before meditating rather than burning it during the entire practice. That way, you get a light hint of the aroma to further enhance the environment rather than a choking cloud of fragrance competing with your mantra.

Bells, chimes, and bowls can also make a nice addition to your meditation space. Sounding a soft chime to signal the start and end of your practice can be yet another way to create a unique neurological association with the meditation practice. I play a singing bowl prior to meditation. I find it helps to soothe my mind and usher in a state of deep tranquility and peace. It sets the tone for my meditation and connects me to the ancient culture from which the practices of meditation arose.

Another helpful recommendation is to let your family, children, partners, or roommates know what you're up to. Inform them of your meditation practice and that you'll be indisposed for the next fifteen to twenty minutes so they don't come looking for you. When your friends and loved ones know and understand what you're doing, they are much more likely to respect your time and leave you alone. You may even consider hanging a sign on the door of your meditation space that says something like "Silence Please—I'm Meditating." With time, they'll come to recognize that you are serious about your practice and support you in staying on track, especially if they notice all the benefits we discussed in previous chapters. Even better—they may ask to join you.

A special note here about pets. If you have dogs or cats it's not uncommon that your pets may find you *incredibly interesting* when you meditate. I'm guessing this is due to the fact that dogs and cats lack the endless subtext of linguistically structured thought we humans have and are by nature much more intimately connected to the field of consciousness we discussed earlier. Pets are deeply plugged into the non-local field of awareness and when they sense that their human companions are tapping into that non-local field as well, they want to be closer to them.

Once, several years ago while visiting my brother over a long weekend, I awakened early to do my morning meditation. I had propped myself up on the bed with a few pillows and had been meditating for about ten minutes or so when I heard the door creak open. I opened my eyes slightly to see Belle, my brother's dog, sneak into the room, hop up onto the bed, and curl up in a ball next to me. She remained there, resting against my side for the remainder of the meditation, at which time she sat up, shook her head, and hopped down to the floor.

So don't be surprised if when you meditate your animals seek you out. And yes, you can meditate with your pets, provided they are able to be still and not be a distraction. I have several friends who meditate with their pets and find it deepens their bond with their dog or cat. Otherwise, if your animal has difficulty settling down, it may be best to put them in another room where they won't disturb you. As a side note, one of my friends and fellow meditation instructor Amanda Ree, has built a business around teaching Ayurvedic well-being for dogs, including meditations specifically designed to be practiced with your dog. For additional information, visit www.samadog.com.

It's important to remember that meditation is an internal process—we're taking our attention inward. Therefore, any of the externals mentioned previously—such as location, bells, chimes, candles, icons, or altars—are meant to potentially enhance your practice but are by no means required. I share them as options to test out and see if they are useful for you. You can have an incredibly successful meditation practice with nothing but a chair in your living room or office.

Students often ask if they can meditate outside, and my answer is always yes—but with a few caveats. Sitting in a tranquil natural setting, deeply absorbed in meditation brings to mind images of the Buddha under the Bodhi Tree or ancient Indian sages meditating at the foot of the Himalayas. But in our modern world your experience might be a little different. Remember again that we're guiding our awareness inward and when we're outdoors there can be lots of distractions competing for our attention. Unlike meditating indoors, we're not in a controlled environment so we're potentially going to be exposed to changes in temperature, insects, the sounds of airplanes, cars, animals, or sirens, and the possibility of someone stumbling upon you in your tranquil meditation spot. There's nothing wrong with any of this and it provides us with ample opportunity to come back to the mantra again and again. Meditating outdoors can be a wonderful experience for some, but for others, it's not their cup of tea. As with nearly all these recommendations, see what works best for you. One additional point: if you do choose to meditate outdoors, avoid sitting in the direct sunlight, and try to find a shady area where the sun won't be beating down on you, potentially making you uncomfortable or sunburned.

Now that we've discussed the externals, all that remains is to sit down, get comfortable, and begin to practice. However, one additional suggestion I would make prior to starting to meditate, is to take a few minutes to practice some form of conscious breathing exercise. Whether it's simply deep belly breathing or one of the more well-known pranayama exercises, steady and focused breathing helps to prime the nervous system for meditation and signals the mind and body for deep relaxation. Two to three minutes usually serves as the perfect prelude for a meditation session. (We'll go into more detail about breathing exercises in an upcoming chapter.)

POSITION AND POSTURE

As we are aware, the so-hum meditation is performed in a seated position with eyes closed, but let's take a closer look at how to sit for an optimal meditation session.

As always, the most important guideline is to be comfortable. Comfort can be a subjective experience, so remember what's comfortable for one person may not be for another. But in general, it's a good idea to sit as upright as comfortably possible. This doesn't necessarily mean keeping your spine ramrod straight. While having a super-straight spine may be a component of some more advanced meditation schools, I don't find this approach terribly effective for the average person for two reasons: 1) you have to keep a certain amount of your attention on your posture, which keeps your awareness in your body/mind, rather than allowing it to slip into the gap and 2) it can be uncomfortable. Now if you can keep a nice tall spine during meditation, by all means, do so. It's just that many people have stiff lower backs, which can make holding an erect posture for fifteen to twenty minutes uncomfortable. I recommend sitting upright as comfortably possible because according to yoga, good posture allows the unimpeded flow of subtle energy through the body, plus it also helps us stay alert and avoid dozing off. If we bend our spine out of the vertical plane by rounding too far forward or reclining too far back, chances are good that we'll fall asleep.

You may sit in a chair, on a sofa, on the floor, on a bed, or wherever else your body can be comfortably and relatively upright. You can also look into meditation stools, cushions, or chairs such as Zafus or Backjacks. You may want to test out any seat or cushion you plan to use on a regular basis to make sure it feels good for your body. Some chairs and couches can be really soft and may swallow you up without necessary support, so feel free to use pillows, cushions, or blankets to prop yourself up as needed. If you sit in a chair, it can be helpful to place both feet flat on the floor or perhaps on a folded blanket or pillow to keep your thighs level.

There are classical yoga positions for meditation such as lotus, thunderbolt, and perfect pose, but unless you can sit in them comfortably, don't force yourself. While these poses may look exotic, the general theme is to create a wide base so the hips are slightly above the knees and the spine is straight. You may want to experiment with different poses to see if any of them are appropriate for your body. Remember, however, there's no point in cramming yourself into an impressive meditation posture if you spend your entire meditation fighting the discomfort in your knees, hips, or back.

Related to these meditative postures is what are known as *mudras* or symbolic hand positions or gestures. Like yoga poses, these hand positions have specific meanings and purposes. If you look up images of the Buddha or any of the Hindu deities, you will undoubtedly some of these hand gestures. According to the esoteric teachings of yoga and Buddhism, mudras channel the body's subtle energy flow to bring about specific effects in the mind and body. For example, touching the index finger to the thumb while extending the remaining three fingers is a mudra used to help sharpen memory and concentration. As with the meditation postures, mudras are a matter of personal preference. Feel free to use them if you find them helpful or appropriate, but they are not a required part of your meditation practice. I usually prefer to meditate with my hands cupped together in my lap. You may also rest your palms on your thighs. Traditionally resting your hands palms facing up is considered to be a receptive position, while palms facing down is a grounding position. Try these out and see which you may prefer.

Generally speaking, it's not recommended to lie down during meditation, primarily for the reason that our bodies and nervous system associate lying down with one activity in particular—sleep. Lying down sends a message to your body that it's time for restful dullness, which as we've discussed is different than the restful awareness of meditation. This isn't to say that you can't or shouldn't lie down to meditate. If you're injured or sick, lying down during meditation is perfectly acceptable. When I was thirty years old, I caught chicken pox (not the age I would recommend to get this disease) and I spent the better part of two weeks meditating in a lying position because I was too weak to sit upright for any amount of time. So if you feel more comfortable in a lying position, by all means, lie down. Just be aware that it may be slightly more challenging to stay awake.

Lastly, regarding position and posture, always be willing to adjust your position as necessary. Often during meditation we resist moving or re-positioning our bodies because we feel we're supposed to sit perfectly still for the entire time. This is not only unrealistic but, once again, uncomfortable. As we discussed in the mechanics of stress release, our bodies are likely to settle and let go of stress spontaneously during meditation, so listen to your body and move, scratch, wiggle, shift, or adjust as needed. Furthermore, coughing, sneezing, hiccups, and gurgling stomachs are completely normal experiences to have while meditating. They might seem inconvenient or untimely, but they are part of the human experience, so just like any other thought, notice it, adjust or deal with it as necessary, and then return to the mantra.

MEDITATING WITH OTHERS

Although we discussed the powerful benefits of group meditation in the previous chapter, I want to briefly address meditating with others here. As your personal meditation practice grows, I encourage you to occasionally participate in group meditations. You may notice that the experience of meditating with others can be subtly or noticeably different than meditating alone. The group coherence created by two or more people meditating together can sometimes cultivate a profound stillness or bring about a powerful shift in awareness. Over the years I have participated in several large group meditation courses and events and have found them to be powerful experiences, albeit sometimes difficult to translate into words. For people closely bonded together, meditating together can be a catalyst to deepen the relationship. My wife and I frequently meditate together and afterward we often feel a unique closeness and affinity for each other that is hard to describe and transcends the activities of our everyday relationship.

Whether you meditate with others or by yourself is yet another matter of personal preference. Some of my students have told me how much they love meditating with a group, noting that they can feel a marked difference in the quality of their meditation with others versus when they meditate alone. Others have expressed the exact opposite. It comes down to what works best for you. If you enjoy group meditations, I encourage you to seek out fellow meditators in your area or perhaps start your own neighborhood meditation group. Such groups provide a wonderful opportunity to create localized pockets of focused intentions and higher consciousness.

WHEN AND HOW LONG TO MEDITATE

Two of the most regular questions I get about meditation are, "When is the best time to meditate? And how long should I do it?" Ideally, with this type of practice, it's recommended to meditate twice a day, once in the morning and once again in the early evening. The first meditation is usually practiced right after rising in the morning. This period is usually quiet as the movement of the day hasn't begun to stir up a lot of activity, making it an ideal time to slip into stillness. Once you get up, visit the restroom and perhaps splash some water on you face to make a clean break from sleeping before starting to meditate, rather than just sitting up in bed to practice. The evening meditation is best practiced before dinner, as eating increases the activity of the body. If you meditate after dinner, wait at least an hour to allow your meal to begin digesting before practicing. In this way our meditations are like bookends on the day. We begin our day with the stillness of meditation and then move into activity; then as the day winds down, we enter the stillness again, helping to integrate our activity, and prepare our mind and body for restful sleep.

It's best to meditate *before* vigorous exercise, which will create a lot of energy and activity in the mind and body. You can meditate following a workout, but be sure to give yourself plenty of time to cool down and to come back to a more settled state. A gentle yoga sequence or some light stretching can be practiced before meditation, however. The yoga asanas or poses both prepare the body for sitting in meditation comfortably as well as activate the body's subtle energy systems, which will aid in the removal of stress.

I'm also frequently asked if it's acceptable to meditate before bed. This is a personal preference, but it's generally not recommended to practice just before going to sleep. There are two reasons for this. First, meditation can create a more mentally aware and alert state, which could interfere with falling asleep. Second, if you're trying to meditate after a tiring long day, chances are good you'll fall asleep and not get as much benefit from the practice. In addition, as we touched upon in Chapter 2, we don't want to get into the habit of using meditation as a sleep aid, otherwise our mind and body may become conditioned to fall asleep every time we meditate. If you have had a busy evening but still want to meditate before going to sleep, I would get completely ready for bed (put on your pajamas, go to the bathroom, brush your teeth, etc.) and then meditate for a shortened period, such as five to ten minutes before sliding right under the covers and off to dreamland. In my experience, meditating any time after 8:00 p.m. followed by activity creates too much mental alertness and I'm unable to fall asleep at a regular time. But as with most of these recommendations, test them out and see what works best for you.

How long should you meditate? As a beginner, I would suggest starting with fifteen to twenty minutes of meditation per session. The twenty-minute window seems to be something of a "Goldilocks" zone that feels "just right" for many people. Perhaps that's roughly the amount of time it takes for different brain processes to progressively power down during meditation. Maybe it's the ideal minimum time for the mechanics of stress release to kick in. Regardless, I would suggest making twenty minutes of meditation your minimum goal to strive for initially. I once heard Stuart Wilde, the wonderful author and lecturer mention meditating for twenty-four minutes per session—one minute of meditation for every hour of the day. I like that idea, and I often use twenty-four minutes as my daily benchmark.

Thirty minutes is usually recommended as the upper threshold for the length of daily meditations and is probably the most beneficial amount of time to spend in stillness if you can make it work in your schedule. Can you go longer? Sure, but here's something to consider—when you meditate for prolonged periods it will probably result in the increased release of stress, which may become uncomfortable or make you feel "spaced out." It's for this reason that if you ever choose to attend a prolonged meditation retreat, there will most likely be a staff of volunteers to assist you to help you stay grounded. In that environment, prolonged meditations are fine because you are away from work, families, and other responsibilities, so you can devote more undivided attention to your practice. If you were to attempt that amount of meditation with your daily householder lifestyle, it could be challenging and is, therefore, not typically recommended.

Do you have to meditate twice a day? No, but know that this frequency creates more momentum than a once-daily practice. It surrounds your daily activity in a cocoon of stillness that reinforces your commitment to being a regular meditator. Remember also that it typically takes between twenty-one to thirty days to form a new habit. In the beginning, any new behavior, diet, or exercise program takes a concerted effort to maintain. But as time and practice continues, the new behavior feels increasingly natural, until ultimately when we reach that twenty-one-to-thirty–day period it has become the new normal. Repetition is the mother of all skill and by repeating the new activity, new neurological connections are formed, making what was once difficult easy. This habit-forming mechanism also enlists the body's natural homeostatic balance—what can be thought of as our internal comfort level thermostat. Pushing against the previous status quo will initially feel uncomfortable, but with repeated effort, the thermostat is adjusted to a new setting, a new comfort level.

When I first began to meditate, it was a challenge, even a little struggle to get up a little earlier or postpone dinner to fit in my meditations. But I kept doing it until the new schedule became a part of my life. This is normal for me now, and to not do it simply wouldn't feel right. Just like any new skill, you have to do it until it becomes a part of you. At one time when you were a child you probably resisted having to brush your teeth before bed. But now, after years of doing it, it would feel wrong to not do it. It's the same with meditation. Use the leverage of regular practice to turn meditation into a lifestyle habit that runs on automatic pilot.

Ultimately, consistency in meditation is far more important than quantity. It's better to meditate regularly twice a day for ten minutes at a time than to meditate for thirty minutes once every couple of days. Your mind and body love familiar patterns and rhythms, so set up a meditation time and length that works for you. The recommendations I have shared are the ideal, but you know your lifestyle better than any recommendations in a book. Use the "ww rule"—*whatever works*. If you are committed to a regular meditation practice, I have no doubt that you'll find a way to fit it into your life, in your own way.

DEALING WITH DISTURBANCES

Over the course of your meditation career there will be numerous times when your meditation session is interrupted by disturbances in your environment. This is simply a normal aspect of our practice; external activity will occasionally interfere with the repetition of the mantra, sometimes requiring our attention. I urge you to accept this reality and try not to get hung up on it. If we are settling deep into meditation, relaxing and letting go of stress and there is some interruption that demands our attention, getting upset or emotionally reactive about being disturbed is a step in the wrong direction. Know that they happen and deal with them as necessary.

If a disturbance is something minor, such as a clap of thunder, a car alarm, or a ringing phone, treat the interruption as you would any other thought and just come back to the mantra. In this way, distractions and disturbances become opportunities to strengthen our attention on being mindful in the present moment.

If the disturbance requires your immediate attention, as in the case of a delivery that must be signed for or a pet that needs to go outside, take a moment if possible before getting up to deal with the situation and transition gently into activity. Do what needs to be done and when you've taken care of things, return to your meditation, and complete the remaining time. Again, take care not to become frustrated by any interruption. Notice the situation with a calm attitude of "Oh, how interesting," attend to the matter at hand, or just return to the mantra. It's nothing to get worked up over.

It's also important to have realistic expectations of your environment. If you're meditating in your personal meditation space at home, you will most likely have few potential interruptions; however, if you are meditating on an airplane, for example, your mantra has to contend with the background roar of the engines, announcements from the cockpit, conversations of the other passengers, the beverage cart, and someone bumping into you or kicking your seat. Therefore, these external influences are the "givens" of an airplane meditation session. Accept them as the backdrop of your practice, knowing once again that the real objective is to keep going within.

Over the years I have meditated throughout a wide variety of locations, vehicles, and circumstances—each one with its own unique nuances. I even meditated on a theme park bench just prior to the start of an enormous holiday parade. I was immersed in the clamor of music, parents pushing strollers, laughing children, and the smell of popcorn.

But because I knew where I was and had chosen to meditate there, I couldn't expect the environment to be that of a remote holy shrine in the Himalayas. I allowed it to be what it was and ended up having a grounding and deeply restorative meditation despite the bedlam that surrounded me.

There are occasions, however, when postponing your meditation to another time might be beneficial. If you've encountered an emotionally turbulent situation, such as being involved in an argument or watching a tragic or violent story on the evening news, it would be a good idea to wait a little while for some of the stronger feelings to subside before meditating. And while it may seem self-evident, it's important to note that meditation immediately following the consumption of alcohol is typically not recommended. Since alcohol is a depressant, it will almost certainly make focus on the mantra difficult and will create a feeling of dullness in the mind and body.

As always, remember not to take meditation too seriously. Be easy with yourself and know when to continue your practice and when to save it for another time. Once when my wife and I were meditating together, after about fifteen minutes of practice, we began to hear the soft jingly music of an ice cream truck making its rounds through our neighborhood. I didn't take much notice of it initially; it was just background noise and I continued to bring my attention back to the mantra. But as the truck drove closer, the music got louder, and we soon could recognize the familiar melody of "The Farmer in the Dell" accompanied by the sounds of various barnyard animals. I could hear my wife begin to softly snicker with the sound of each animal until, ultimately, with the duck's "quack," she erupted into a full-blown belly laugh. Although she tried her best to contain it and continue meditating, Pandora's Box had been opened, and we both quickly became infected with laughter. The ice cream truck came and went—mooing, clucking, oinking, and quacking the whole time. Try as we might, my wife and I just couldn't recover the meditation. It was okay though, because we knew when it was time to surrender to the giggles and save our meditation for later.

> *One of the symptoms of an approaching nervous breakdown is the belief that one's work is terribly important.*
>
> —Bertrand Russell

EXPECTATIONS DURING MEDITATION REVISITED

Although we discussed our expectations of meditation in Chapter 2, knowing how to relate to those expectations can make the difference between maintaining a successful practice and quitting. Therefore, these points are worth repeating:

- *Have no agenda.* When you sit down to meditate, don't do so with the intention of "getting something out of it." Meditation is essentially an act of surrendering to the present moment. Holding out for a particular result will only lead to frustration. When we meditate, we are trusting that the process knows what it's doing and will bring us our highest good, even if it doesn't seem that way.

    There have been times when I have been meditating and my mind has been awash with all types of thoughts, which might feel disappointing if I have my heart set on slipping into the gap. However, it never fails that later on during that day I experience some profound stillness, perhaps on my drive to work or during a meeting. Remember, the real value of meditation isn't experienced during the practice itself, but during the rest of your day, often when you least expect it.

    Having no agenda also means resisting the temptation to look for flashy experiences. Might they happen? Perhaps (see below), but we don't sit down to meditate to experience a trance-like, extraordinary far-out trip. Our popular culture, while it has helped draw attention to meditation through film and television, often presents a somewhat fantastical image of meditation and what it does. There's nothing wrong with this; however, for the sake of our practice it's important to stay grounded in what our meditation practice is actually doing for us.

1. *What happens during your meditation is a result of what your body-mind needs at that time.* Our physiology and psychology are incredibly intricate and complex systems of information and energy that are constantly changing. Mind and body shift and transform according to perceptions, changes in the environment, moods, emotions, thoughts, and countless other factors. When you sit down to meditate today, you're meditating with a body and mind that are different in countless ways since your last meditation. Therefore, there's no reason to expect that your experience will be the same as last time. Regardless of what happens, your body-mind is getting exactly what it needs from the experience, and sometimes that's different than what *you* think it needs. Once again, trust that this amazing aggregate of cells, tissues, organs, impulses, thoughts, emotions, and biochemical and bioelectric signals has the intelligence to restore itself to balance in the most optimal and efficient manner.

    It's worth repeating that like a snowflake, each meditation is unique. No two meditations are the same. Even if you meditate at the same time in the same place, day in and day out, the *you* who is meditating is always changing and metabolizing the meditation differently. And that's okay. Once you become comfortable with this truth, it becomes much easier to let go and allow each meditation to be what it will be.

2. *Don't get attached to the scenery.* During meditation, you may have moments that feel special, unique, or somewhat abnormal. You may feel a warm, tingling sensation in your hands or another part of your body, you may have vivid memories

CREATING A SUCCESSFUL MEDITATION PRACTICE 183

or images flash across your mental screen, or you may feel a blissful experience of mental and bodily expansion for which words can do no justice. Since we are, at our core, a field of infinite potential and pure creativity, technically speaking, pretty much anything can happen. But what's important to keep in mind is that all those things, as interesting or curious as they may be, are essentially scenery on a larger journey of awakening.

Imagine taking a drive from Orlando to Tampa. (If you're not familiar with Florida roadways, the primary route between these two cities is Interstate 4 or I4. This roughly sixty- to ninety-minute stretch of highway contains no shortage of billboard signs of all shapes and sizes.) On this imaginary drive, consider what would happen if we pulled the car over at every billboard to stop and study it. Each sign becomes more interesting than the last, and before you know it, we never make it to Tampa. This is what can happen in meditation. Those unique experiences can sometimes become distractions that sidetrack us from the destination. This doesn't mean we shouldn't savor those experiences if they happen; we just don't want to get stuck in them.

The Zen Buddhist Master Linji Yixuan once said, "If you meet the Buddha on the road, kill him." Sounds rather drastic, doesn't it? Actually, this phrase has a symbolic meaning—it is a reminder that whatever our conception of some exalted higher state of consciousness might be (whether that's a vision, an epiphany, or some supernormal experience), it's ultimately not the true reality. "Kill the Buddha" means get rid of the false image and move along; in other words, get back to the practice. In some schools of thought, special, otherworldly experiences are sometimes called "spiritual traps" because they can seem so compelling and captivating. In our case when those special experiences occur, we know what to do—come back to the mantra.

TIMING YOUR MEDITATION

Should you use a timer for your meditations? This is a personal choice that has some practical considerations to take into account. For those of us householders who have responsibilities, things to do, and places to go, using a meditation timer might be a helpful way to make sure we don't spend too much time drifting in meditation while other areas of our lives suffer. For example, I rise at around 5:00 a.m. every morning and meditate shortly after. Using a timer helps me to both stay on track with my morning schedule as well as keep me set on a consistent amount of meditation time. A timer can also be a good tool to keep us from falling asleep during our meditations. After a long day at work, my evening meditations can occasionally relax my mind and body to the point of drifting off to sleep. Using a timer assists me in returning to wakefulness rather than la-la land when I'm done.

With that said, don't feel as if you have to use a timer. You can always occasionally open your eyes to take a quick glimpse at a clock or watch to check the time. However, with regular and consistent practice, your body-mind will begin to adjust to a consistent length of time in meditation. If you meditate for fifteen minutes every day, your system will eventually recognize this period of time and spontaneously return to wakeful activity on its own. To reinforce this process, take a quick look at the time prior to your meditation and have the subtle intention to meditate for a set period at the end of which you will automatically end your meditation. I have had the experience on several occasions of doing this and to my amazement, I often open my eyes *at the exact minute I had intended to stop.* Mind you, I wasn't trying to calculate how long I had been meditating and predict when to stop. I would sometimes have the thought, "I wonder if I should stop now" or "Am I done yet," but I would just return to the mantra and whenever I did open my eyes, it was right on time, almost as if being directed by some internal guidance.

If you do decide to use a timer, the key to remember is to use one that has a soft and gentle chime or bell. I don't recommend using a kitchen or egg timer. In addition to the relentless tick, tick, tick, tick that doesn't exactly contribute to creating an environment free of distractions, the bell can be loud and jarring. Remember, the practice of meditation is to gently withdraw ourselves from activity to stillness, like a decrescendo in music, getting softer and softer. Likewise, when we return from meditation to activity, it should be like a calm crescendo back into movement. A sharp or piercing sound can startle us from a deeply settling meditation practice, lurching us back to the waking state instead of softly coaxing ourselves back to the world of thoughts and movements.

I've been using a meditation app on my phone for several years called Insight Timer. It is an excellent tool for timing my meditations. You can set multiple meditations for varying lengths of time; end your meditation with a variety of bells, bowls, chimes and gongs; set interval bells; or listen to guided meditations. It also has a social aspect that allows you to see how many people are meditating with the app at any given time, make friends, and send messages to your fellow meditators. Last, it tracks the length of each meditation, logs each session so you can measure your progress over time, and gives you reward notifications when you reach milestones. Now, I don't want to get too far lost in promoting the virtue of app timers as they are ultimately externals that aren't required to practice meditation. However, they can make timing your meditations, keeping track of them, and staying motivated easier. For example, if you're only three days away from meditating one hundred days straight, you're probably more likely to keep going to hit that goal and stay on track.

Using a timer is entirely up to you. Experiment with meditating with and without to see what works best in your life. There's no need to go all out; most cell phones now include a timer function that has a soft bell that will work well.

COMPLETING YOUR MEDITATION

So now we've covered nearly all the essential details for creating a successful meditation practice. Only one aspect remains: how to end your meditation. This may seem like a minor point; after all, couldn't we just open our eyes and get back to business?

Well, yes, you could do that, but remember, what we're trying to do here is set ourselves up for a successful, long-lasting, and fulfilling meditation practice. And this final aspect can help you get the most from your practice. Therefore, we'll sum up concluding your meditation in the following four key points.

1. **Stop thinking the mantra.** When either your timer rings or you decide to end your meditation simply stop repeating the mantra. After having played it in your mind for ten to twenty minutes or more, your mind may want to hang onto it, so make a clean break and let the mantra fade away completely.
2. **Sit comfortably for a few minutes with your eyes closed.** *This is important.* Take some time to simply be. Allow the stillness and silence to sink in. No matter what you experienced during meditation, taking this time allows your body-mind to integrate the experience. Even if you dozed off and slept through the entire meditation, take a minute or two to absorb and reset.
3. **Take a deep breath and slowly allow your eyes to float open.** Slowly look around; perhaps wiggle you fingers or toes and gently begin to introduce movement back into your body. If it feels appropriate, bring your palms together to your heart and take a small bow in gratitude for the meditation and its benefits. Slowly begin to return to your daily activity, but see if you can carry some of the stillness of meditation with you into the rest of your

day. Try to nurture the calmness of meditation and avoid the temptation to jump right into vigorous action. The activity of life will re-assert itself soon enough; there's no need to give it any additional help.
4. **Remember this post meditation rule.** *There is no running to or from meditation.* Approach and leave each meditation with a sense of calmness and reverence for the stillness you are cultivating.

These guidelines can be summed up in three words: *Take your time*. Ending your meditation shouldn't be rushed. The post-meditation period is a delicate time, so move with gentleness, ease, and deliberate mindfulness as you get back into the business of life. If you've ever taken a yoga class, the final pose is often Savasana or Corpse Pose. This pose is meant to be a transition zone between the movement, breathing, strength, balance, and flexibility of the yoga session and our normal daily activity. It serves as a resting period of integration during which the experience of the practice is metabolized into our lives before we return to the world. In the same way, by pausing following our meditation, we give our mind and body the opportunity for the stillness to take hold.

It's keenly important to return to activity slowly, so much so that if you don't have enough time to gently transition out of meditation, it would be better to shorten the actual length of the meditation so you can take the necessary additional minutes to capture the calm of meditation. Doing so will help to treasure the stillness you accessed during meditation as your most precious and valued resource.

As we end this chapter on creating a successful meditation practice, remember that these guidelines are meant to be *recommendations* that can help set you up for success as a meditator. They shouldn't be thought of as hard-and-fast rules that can never be violated. No one knows your schedule, routine, comfort level, and tendencies better than you. It's important to do what feels the most natural and comfortable for you. If not, you'll most likely quit and then think that you're a failure at meditation or that you're just not cut out for it. Trust me: *You are cut out for it*. I believe that everyone can meditate if they learn it properly and have the freedom to fit the practice into their own lifestyle. Your meditation practice is just that—*yours*. It's as individual as your fingerprint. Especially in the beginning, it's important to find the right rhythm, cadence, and frequency of your practice. Like I tell my yoga students, we don't try to force our bodies into a specific yoga posture; instead, we adapt the pose to suit our unique body type and limitations. It's the same with meditation. Tailor it to fit your needs, not the other way around. Like a new pair of shoes, once broken in and contoured to your feet, they will carry you for miles and miles.

Lastly, remember the more you do it, the more natural it will become. Consistency is key. Habits take time to form, but once they do, they become a way of life. Consider implementing the 21/90 rule, which states that habits begin to form after roughly twenty-one days of practice and after ninety days, the habit becomes a part of your lifestyle. What was once difficult becomes easy. Meditate for thirty days and what was once challenging will become routine; meditate for one hundred days and the practice will become a part of who you are.

Learned properly and practiced regularly, meditation will be the best habit you could ever form.

> *You are what your deepest desire is. As is your desire, so is your intention. As is your intention, so is your will. As is your will, so is your deed. As is your deed, so is your destiny.*
>
> —The Upanishads

CHAPTER 9

TAKING YOUR PRACTICE DEEPER

By now you've hopefully had the opportunity to practice meditation several times. You've learned the benefits, understood the technical details, and explored how to personalize your practice. You may be wondering though: What comes next? In this chapter I'd like to discuss a few "optional extras" to help enhance your practice and go deeper into the richness of meditation. Please know that you already possess everything you need to enjoy a lifetime of full and rewarding meditation. What I offer here are additional suggestions, ideas, and techniques that you may find helpful on your path. They are in no way required, but if you find them useful or beneficial in your practice, feel free to incorporate them in a way that is comfortable for you.

THE SEVEN SPIRITUAL LAWS OF SUCCESS

Deepak Chopra's bestselling book *The Seven Spiritual Laws of Success*, has been a mainstay of my library since it was published in 1994.[1] This small and concise book explains the way in which the unmanifest becomes manifest through seven fundamental principles or laws operating at the heart of nature. They are a means to understand success beyond the material level of "having and doing" and struggle or hard work. While it may sound like a catchy self-help title, this book represents the foundational principles of the yoga and Vedanta philosophy, principles that are both common sense and profound in their understanding.

Through proper application of these principles, we can more easily align our lives with the laws of nature to achieve happiness, abundance, and the fulfillment of our life's purpose. I've come to think of these principles as the instruction manual for living a happy, fulfilling, abundant, and profoundly spiritual life. Like the operating system for a computer, they provide the guidelines for discovering our unlimited human potential. It's a book I can't recommend highly enough as a foundational tool for people of all ages and backgrounds to profoundly explore their true self and achieve their desires. I strongly encourage you to get your own copy so as to get the most out of these teachings.

In my experience and practice of these principles, I have found them to be deeply woven into the practice of meditation. Each law gives an additional perspective into how our practice of meditation works and, in turn, our meditation expands our understanding of the laws, creating a complementary feedback loop of increasing awareness. Let's briefly explore each law to see how they specifically relate to meditation.

1. **The Law of Pure Potentiality.** This law is essentially a reminder of our true identity as a field of awareness. We are each pure spirit, soul, or consciousness. Like waves or eddies on the ocean, we are expressions of that infinite field of conscious intelligence, creativity, and bliss. We are connected with everyone and everything in an unbounded, infinite, and eternal field of silent awareness and infinite possibilities.

    Our practice of meditation is governed by the law of pure potentiality—during meditation, our awareness expands and merges into the non-local field of pure spirit. The gap is the field of spirit—beyond time, space, and limitations of cause and effect. Through regular meditation, we tap into this law and infuse our lives with the attributes of spirit: infinity, immortality, unboundedness, timelessness, peace, joy, and bliss.

2. **The Law of Giving and Receiving.** The law of giving and receiving explains that in living systems, energy is always moving and that circulation of this energy is what sustains life and abundance. Energy doesn't sit still, it needs to move, and in keeping that energy flowing through giving and receiving, we nourish the entire universe. To stop or interfere with the flow of energy leads to stagnation and decay. To receive those things we seek, we must be willing to graciously give and sustain the current of life force energy in our lives.

    During meditation, our thoughts arise and fade; they are in a state of perpetual flow. Our job as meditators is to allow them to come and go, receive them without resistance, and let them move on or "give" them back to the mind field from where they arose. Holding onto a thought obstructs the current, in effect damming up the stream and creating a "thought logjam." Give and receive the thoughts in a state of innocent witnessing and allow them to flow through you unimpeded.

3. **The Law of Karma or Cause and Effect**. While the law of giving and receiving is about the circulation of life-energy, the law of karma is about the *content or quality* of that energy. The word *karma* means "action" but also implies the consequences of that action. When we make positive or uplifting choices (thoughts, words, actions) for everyone potentially affected by that choice, the more positive and uplifting the consequences of that choice will be. This law is all about making conscious choices and being aware of the effects of our actions. Conscious choices are those that invoke our free will; unconscious choices are mindless autopilot actions that don't even feel like choices—they seem to happen entirely on their own.

    As it relates to meditation, through our practice, we create more awareness, more space, and more opportunities to witness, notice, and make the most evolutionary choices. In addition, as we continue to enter the stillness between our thoughts, we are able to transcend our karma. It's as if we are repeatedly washing a dirty cloth in a stream; with each washing a few more stains are lifted, until ultimately all impurities are removed.

4. **The Law of Least Effort.** This law informs us that the guiding principle of accomplishment in nature is effortless ease. Nature is carefree, abundant, harmonious, and nourishing. It embodies that idea of "doing less, and accomplishing more." Whether in the flight of birds, the swimming of fish, the growing of a flower, or the playing of children, nature embodies economy of motion in all she does. When we tap into this "flow" of life we can *do less, and everything gets done.*

    In our meditation practice, the entire process is an act of least effort. Tapping into stillness requires we accept and surrender to this moment as it is, effortlessly repeating our mantra lightly and innocently. Going beyond our thoughts is not a process of force or struggle; it is about timing, finesse, and letting go. Only when we release and soften our focus will the doors to higher awareness swing open.

5. **The Law of Intention and Desire.** This principle is based upon the understanding that the universe is a field of energy and information and this field is influenced by intention. Intention is a force of nature that triggers the fulfillment of all our desires. Just as a seed contains all the instructions and processes required to grow a tree, in the same way each of our intentions contain the blueprints and mechanisms for their fulfillment. Our role is not to understand the "how's" of manifestation; the intention itself contains all the steps involved in making something happen. We need only be clear about our intentions and that they help to serve the evolutionary will of the universe.

    To harness the power of intention during meditation, become aware of your intentions and desires. By reviewing what you wish to manifest in your life prior to going into meditation, you are choosing the seeds you wish to sow. As you begin your meditation practice, you release those intentions into the still field of pure awareness from where they are able to blossom in their own season.

Meditation also cultivates the awareness to notice the clues and synchronicities that indicate your intentions are being fulfilled. These hints are often subtle, so the heightened awareness fostered by meditation helps us catch signals from the non-local realm of spirit that might otherwise go unnoticed.

6. **The Law of Detachment.** The law of detachment reminds us that clinging, grasping, and attachment are fundamental causes of suffering, and that true fulfillment and enjoyment of life can only be found by embracing detachment. Attachment is clinging to the known, which is our past conditioning that keeps us locked in rigid patterns of thought and behavior. It's an act of insecurity and fear that locks us in a prison of past beliefs and ideals. Detachment on the other hand, liberates us into the field of all possibilities. We can step confidently into the unknown, trusting that in a world of perpetual impermanence and change, uncertainty is not something to be feared, but rather a source of great strength and security.

To give a personal example of this principle in action, let me share a story from my childhood. In June 1977, my family and I were on a trip to see our relatives in Michigan. During that visit, my parents decided to take me and my brother to see a movie. We headed off to the local mall where my brother and I had our hearts set on seeing the newly released Disney movie, *Herbie Goes to Monte Carlo*. Unknown to us however, our parents had other plans.

Once we got to the theater, our parents told us that they decided we were going to see *another* movie. This news promptly triggered a white-hot meltdown from my brother and me. We had been looking forward to *Herbie* for weeks and our parents knew it. They changed the rules and we were the special kind of angry that only a ten and nine year old could be when they didn't get their way.

Out of fear that Matt and I would make a scene, our parents sternly told us to "Pipe down, or you won't see *any* movie," as they purchased the tickets for the "other" film. I don't remember if they told us the name of the thing or not, and even if they did, it probably couldn't have made a dent in the seething anger Matt and I were feeling.

A few minutes later I was pouting next to my brother in the darkened theater, unable to care less about what we were about to watch. The film began and I heard a faint drumroll . . . 20th Century something on the screen . . . and then darkness. And then, on a black background appeared ten blue words: *A long time ago in a galaxy far, far away . . .*

Herbie who?

Do I even need to continue?

This is how attachment works. In wanting things to be a certain way *so badly*, we often block out something absolutely incredible that sits right in front of us. It's as if our attachment puts a pair of blinders on us and we can only see one way to go, when in reality, an infinity of options exist.

For my brother and me, our attachment to *Herbie Goes to Monte Carlo* shut out all other possibilities. Fortunately, my ten-year-old attachment was no match for *Star Wars* (And in case you're wondering, one day many years later, I eventually did see *Herbie Goes to Monte Carlo*. My parents made the right decision.)

To bring this back to meditation, the law of detachment is an ever-present reminder to let go of attachment to expectations or a specific result. Every meditation is uniquely perfect for your mind and body at that time. Chasing after some ideal experience only robs you of the boundless wonder of the present moment. You never know what possibilities exist during your practice, so relax, detach, and trust the process.

7. **The Law of Dharma or Purpose in Life.** The Sanskrit word *dharma* means purpose in life, or what you specifically came here to do. You have a unique gift or talent to give to the world, something you can do unlike anyone else in the world. There are no spare pieces in the cosmos and no one can do what you do in the special way you do it.

    The root word of dharma also means "to uphold," which implies that by performing your dharma, you help to support the entire universe in its growth and evolution. Therefore, it's crucial that you give genuine consideration to why you're here and what you've come to do.

    Through meditation, we discover that the mind's dharma is to expand into ever higher states of awareness. The mind is destined to experience *atma darshan* (glimpsing the soul), *cosmic consciousness* (experiencing local and non-local awareness simultaneously), *divine consciousness* (the witnessing awareness existing within both subjects and objects of consciousness), and *unity consciousness* (the end of separation; the merging of the individual with the universal). All these levels of awareness are hard-wired into your consciousness and exist within you as your spiritual birthright. By tapping into the stillness of meditation, you activate the mind's dharma and allow it to reach its full potential. Through this law, therefore, we discover the highest goal and purpose of meditation—the evolution of our consciousness toward enlightenment.

    By understanding these laws, you open an untapped reservoir of insight and knowledge that will continue to deepen your meditation practice. I encourage you to not only review the brief explanation offered here, but to also explore *The Seven Spiritual Laws of Success* in its entirety to fully grasp the principles and make them a regular part of your daily life.

BREATHING PRACTICE

> *The process of breathing, if fully understood and experienced in its profound significance, could teach us more than all the philosophies of the world.*
> —Lama Govinda

Another tool to help you deepen your meditation practice is yogic breathing. Known as *pranayama* in Sanskrit, yogic breathing is an entire science and art unto itself. *Prana* means vital essence or primordial life force energy. It is the subtle energy that animates your body and the fundamental creative impulse of all living things. Prana flows and circulates throughout nature and within your body. It is a carrier of energy and information and is a vital component of the air we inhale thousands of times each day. Pranayama, therefore, is the management and regulation of our life force energy through breathing.

As we discovered in Chapter 2, there is no clear separation between our mind and body; therefore, our breathing maintains an intimate relationship with all layers of our being. The breath is the dynamic bridge between our body and mind. We breathe between 17,000–23,000 breaths per day; the way in which we breathe deeply influences our energy levels, moods, emotions, and overall state of mind. The breath mirrors the activity of your mind; when your mind is racing and turbulent, your breathing is shallow, rapid, and chaotic. Likewise, when your mind is calm and settled, your breathing is deep, slow, and steady. However, this mirroring works both ways; rapid breathing generates increased mental activity, while slow, calm breathing helps to still mental turbulence.

The ancient yogis were keenly aware of this fact and devised specific breathing techniques to influence their mental and physical states. These techniques are easily learned and can help to prepare the mind and body for periods of meditation. What follows are five classic yogic breathing exercises. I practice one or two of these techniques each day to help set the stage for my meditation session. I recommend that you try each technique once or twice before integrating into your meditation routine. As with meditation itself, always move toward comfort when practicing these exercises. Listen to the signals your body is sending you. If it doesn't feel right, or if you feel lightheaded or woozy, stop the exercise or come back to it at another time. If you have any additional concerns, please speak with your health care provider before attempting these exercises.

Before you start—

- Each of these techniques are meant to be practiced by inhaling and exhaling through the nose. By breathing through our nose, we take advantage of several key physiological benefits. First, nose breathing warms the air as it passes into our lungs, making for a smoother temperature transition when taking deep breaths. Second, the nose is our primary air filter; the hairs and mucus membranes of the nasal passages sift out airborne contaminants, dust, germs, and bacteria. The mouth doesn't have this ability, allowing impurities direct access into our lungs. Finally, our bodies seem to intuitively fill our lungs more fully when we breathe through the nose. When we mouth breathe, we tend to breathe into the chest only. But when we breathe through the nose, the air penetrates deeper, filling our lungs more deeply.

- For each exercise, try to place the tip of your tongue right behind your front top two teeth. You'll find a little ridge there that some traditions refer to as *fire point*. Placing the tip of your tongue in this position is said to close a subtle energy circuit that keeps the prana or life force from leaking during pranayama practice. If that seems too esoteric or far out to grasp, the second, more practical benefit of fire point is that it helps to relax the face, neck, and jaw. If you have the tendency to clench your jaw or hold tension in your facial muscles, fire point is a great way to help reduce that stress, and since we want our faces to be relaxed during our breathing exercises, it's a great habit to get into.

Natural Belly Breathing
As strange as it may sound, few of us actually breathe "naturally." Most of us breathe by raising our chest and shoulders, huffing and puffing, and using an unnecessary amount of effort. This type of breathing is often a byproduct of the stress response that keeps our bodies in a perpetually tense and rigid state. We therefore rely on force and may even strain to fill our lungs.

Natural breathing is the exact opposite. It's spontaneous and fluid, free from struggle or tension. Imagine a baby lying in her crib. Her breathing is soft and easy; as she breathes, her belly rises up and down. Her shoulders and chest are relaxed and the breath rides in and out like gentle waves lapping the shore. This is how our bodies were meant to breathe—with maximum efficiency and least effort. Anatomically speaking, the diaphragm, a large dome-shaped muscle at the base of our ribcage, draws downward as we inhale creating a vacuum in our lungs. This vacuum sucks the air in through our nostrils or mouth and fills our lungs. The downward draw of the diaphragm causes the belly to expand outward, hence the name *belly breathing*. The diaphragmatic movement uses less energy than heaving the shoulders and chest up and down; but, even more importantly, diaphragmatic breathing fills the lungs more completely.

Typically, our lungs have a total capacity of approximately 6,000 milliliters. Unfortunately, the average breath is only about 500 milliliters! That means that for most of us, we are taking in nowhere near the total volume of air that our lungs can hold. Fortunately, through natural belly breathing and the additional exercises explained below, we can greatly increase our lung capacity and the amount of mind-clearing, body-healing prana we can absorb.

To perform belly breathing, sit in a comfortable position with your spine upright. Place one hand on your lower abdomen near your navel and the other hand on the center of your chest near where your collar bones come together. Close your eyes and put your attention on your abdomen. Take a deep breath and expand your abdomen outward, pushing it toward your hand. As you exhale, collapse your belly back toward your spine. Repeat this cycle noticing your lower hand riding the expansions and contraction of your abdomen. Your upper hand shouldn't be moving; it is there simply as a check to make sure your chest remains still and doesn't rise or fall.

Natural belly breathing can be performed at any time for as long as it is comfortable. The more frequently you practice it the more second nature it will be to you. Eventually, it will become your default way to breathe, and that's a good thing as it will help you have greater lung capacity, more energy, and increased relaxation. As applied to meditation practice, natural belly breathing is a wonderful prelude to meditation. Just two or three minutes of deep abdominal breathing sends a calming wave of relaxation through your entire body. Deep breathing exercises such as this activate the parasympathetic (or rest-and-digest) nervous system and begin to down-regulate the stress response, paving the way for a deep meditation. Try adding a few minutes before your next meditation session and take note of how it creates a soothing transition from dynamic activity into the stillness of meditation.

Belly breathing is the foundation of the remaining pranayama techniques. Learn and practice it frequently to gain the greatest benefit. It also provides a calming backdrop for *the soul questions*, a technique we will explore in detail in an upcoming section.

The Bellows Breath

The second breathing technique is known in Sanskrit as *bhastrika*, or bellows breath. This is an invigorating and cleansing breath that helps to stoke the inner fire known as *agni* in Ayurveda. It generates energy and warmth while clearing the mind.

To perform the bellows breath, sit comfortably with an upright spine. Relax any tension in your neck or shoulders and place your attention in your lower abdomen. Take a few deep belly breaths, inhale fully through your nose, and then forcefully and rapidly exhale completely by drawing your abdomen in toward your spine. Immediately inhale sharply to complete the breath and repeat, taking about one second per cycle. The movement of the breath is produced entirely from your diaphragm. Your shoulders, neck, and chest should remain relaxed and steady as your abdomen moves in and out. Begin with a round of twenty breaths and then pause for a few moments to notice how your body feels. After about thirty seconds, perform a second round of forty breaths, followed by a short break, and then a final round of sixty breaths. Between each round breathe normally and notice the sensations in your body. If you feel uncomfortable, lightheaded, or tingling in your body, discontinue your practice and return to it at a later time.

I use the bellows breath each day prior to my morning meditation. It helps me clear my head and shake off any heaviness from sleeping. I find it to be a great way to power-up my system before meditation so I can remain awake and alert and avoid nodding back off to sleep. You can use the bellows breath at any time during the day when you would like a natural boost of energy and mental clarity. However, I recommend avoiding this technique after around 7:00 p.m. as the energy generated may make it difficult to fall asleep.

The Success or Sounding Breath
Known in Sanskrit as *ujjayi*, this breath has a deeply calming effect on both mind and body. It helps to reduce irritation, frustration, and mental turbulence. It focuses the mind, boosts cardiorespiratory function, and is one of the most well-known pranayama techniques for helping us achieve success in all areas of our lives. Indeed, ujjayi is often translated as "to become victorious" or "leading to success." It is also known as the sounding breath due to the audible quality of breathing that sounds somewhat like the waves on the ocean.

To perform the success breath, sit comfortably and take a full deep inhalation in through your nose and exhale through your mouth, making a "haaah" sound. Imagine that you are trying to fog a mirror with your breath. Now repeat the same process, but this time with your mouth closed. You should hear a noticeable rushing sound, like a soft snore. Inhale through your nose, maintaining the same constricted throat position. You should make a similar sound on both the inhalation and exhalation.

The ujjayi breath is another great technique to practice as a transition from activity into stillness. Performing ten rounds prior to meditation will help you unplug from the daily hustle and bustle, and begin to deeply sooth your nervous system in preparation for meditation. It's also a helpful tool to use whenever you feel tense or stressed throughout the day.

Balanced Breathing
The next technique is known as balanced breathing. Balanced breathing can be found in several different traditions, and as the name suggests, it refers to a practice in which we are harmonizing or synching the four stages of our breath (inhalation, retention, exhalation, and retention) together. During our regular activity, our breathing rhythms

vary depending on the activity we're engaged in and the ratio of the breathing stages is rarely, if ever, balanced. As a general rule, during the inhalation of breath, our heart rate and blood pressure rises slightly, and when we exhale, both markers are lowered. During balanced breathing we give equal time to each phase of the breathing cycle. This helps to regulate multiple mind/body systems and create an equilibrium of heart rate, respiration, and blood pressure. It helps to calm and focus the mind while simultaneously slowing the breathing into a steady and even pattern.

To start balanced breathing, sit or stand comfortably. Exhale all the air from your lungs. Now inhale slowly through your nose to a steady count of four (use the belly breathing previously described to ensure you are filling your lungs deeply). Once your lungs are full, hold your breath in for a count of four. Next, slowly and deliberately exhale to a count of four. Hold once again with your lungs empty for a count of four and begin the cycle again. It may take a few cycles to match up your lung capacity, breathing rate, and counts together, but with a little practice, it should become a steady and settling process. I recommend starting with this 4/4/4/4 ratio, but as you practice and your lung capacity increases, you may wish to increase to a 5/5/5/5 ratio. Similarly, if the four count is uncomfortable, feel free to reduce the cycle to three seconds per stage. The goal is to maintain an evenly balanced pace throughout your entire breathing cycle, regardless of the length.

Try five to ten rounds of balanced breathing prior to beginning meditation. The added benefit of this practice is that by paying attention to the count of the breath, your mind is focused on one point, not unlike the mantra. The count serves as a pattern interrupt that brings you back to what you're doing right now—breathing. When you begin your meditation practice, therefore, your mind has already begun to settle, thanks to the calming effects of the balanced breathing. Balanced breathing can also be used in multiple non-meditating applications, for example, sitting in traffic, before a meeting, waiting in line, or prior to

TAKING YOUR PRACTICE DEEPER

exercise are all great opportunities to nourish balance between body and mind.

Alternate Nostril Breathing

The final breathing technique is alternate nostril breathing or *nadi shodhana*. Nadi Shodhana means *channel clearing breath*. In this breath, we manually close off one nostril while breathing through the other. This has a soothing effect and helps to harmonize the left and right hemispheres of the brain while clearing the subtle energy channels within the body. It creates a grounding effect that is effective in settling the mind prior to meditation as well as reducing the mental turbulence of anxiety or insomnia.

To practice alternate nostril breathing, sit comfortably and extend your right arm in front of you. Bend the elbow so your palm is in front of your face. Rest your index and middle finger between your eyebrows (your thumb on one side and your ring finger and pinkie on the other side will toggle to alternately close off your nostrils). Inhale deeply, close off your right nostril with your thumb, and exhale through your left nostril. Keeping your right nostril closed, inhale through your left nostril. At the top of the inhalation, close off the left nostril with your ring and pinkie fingers, lift your thumb, and exhale through the right nostril. Now inhale through the right nostril. Upon full inhalation, close the right nostril again and repeat the cycle. The pattern should look like this: exhale left, inhale left; switch nostrils, exhale right, inhale right; switch nostrils.

I suggest performing five to seven rounds of alternate nostril breathing prior to meditation whenever your mind is feeling extra turbulent or anxious. If comfortable, you can work up to five to ten minutes. Upon completion, pause briefly and notice the effects on your mind and body. With regular practice, you will find that *nadi shodhana* makes an ideal complement to your meditation practice.

While the pranayama exercises described here are all a great supplement to your meditation practice, they are meant to be used *before*—not *during*—your practice. When we're meditating, we're not attempting to control or manipulate our breathing in any way. We just allow it to be natural and effortless, almost as if we forget it's there.

You may be wondering: Which breathing exercise should I use? I've provided several pranayama techniques so you can see what will work best for you. You may find the effects between some of the practices to be similar; however, each form of breathwork contains its own subtle nuances that have to be experienced to be appreciated. Test them out and find the one or two that most noticeably benefit your practice.

DEEP QUESTIONS

If you recall from the introduction, a turning point in my life came when I was faced with some profound questions about the nature of my reality. The questions "Who am I," "What do I want," "Why am I here," and "What makes me truly happy" were profound, consciousness-rattling inquiries that threw my teenage self for a loop. And with good reason. These are some of the most foundational, ontological questions you can ask of yourself. We could think of them as *existential questions* in that they force us to confront the deepest and most mysterious aspects of what it means to be human. At the Chopra Center, they are known as the *soul questions*. By regularly reflecting and probing their meaning, they become a bridge between the local (mind, body, ego, material) domain of consciousness and the non-local (personal, collective, and universal levels of soul and spirit) domain. Let's take a closer look at each of these heavy-hitters and then we'll see how we can integrate them into our meditation practice.

TAKING YOUR PRACTICE DEEPER

Who Am I?

This question challenges us to explore our identity beyond the conventional frames of reference we typically use to define ourselves. It's a question we all ask at one time or another, but we often only give it a few minutes of dedicated thought before moving on to something more practical and down to earth. However, it could be that this question holds the answer to life's deepest mysteries and we owe it to ourselves not to give up so easily.

Most of us usually identify ourselves with our positions and possessions in life. We think of ourselves in terms of the roles we play and the stuff we have:

- I'm a Philadelphian.
- I'm a high school science teacher.
- I'm a father.
- I'm a runner.
- I drive a hybrid car.
- I live in a three-bedroom house in the suburbs.
- I am a Buddhist.
- I'm a performer in a local theater group.

From just this short example, we can form an image of "who this person is" in the traditional sense. But are these labels the real you? Who is the one reading these words in this moment? Who or what is that presence? Try this exercise: Find two photographs of yourself, one recently taken and one from ten to twenty years ago. Look into your own eyes in both pictures. Who is that? Notice that in both pictures your body has changed, but the "you" behind your eyes is the same. The objects of your consciousness (body, time, place, etc.) are different, but the observer or watcher remains consistent through time and space. By asking yourself this question regularly, you begin to shift your identity from the objects of your experience to the one having the experience—your true self.

What Do I Want?

The second question probes the nature of our desires. Understanding what we want tells us a great deal about what matters to us, flushing out more details of our soul. According to the great Vedic texts known as the *Upanishads*, "You are what your deepest desire is. As is your desire, so is your intention. As is your intention, so is your will. As is your will, so is your deed. As is your deed, so is your destiny." When you make contact with what you want, you illuminate the prime movers of your life and the direction it will take.

There are different levels of desire, each valid, depending on your level of consciousness. Consider the following types of desires in your own life:

- Base desires: Intentions for health, nourishment, safety, and security
- Relationship desires: Intentions for nourishing relationships, sexual fulfillment, familial, fraternal, or professional relationships
- Achievement desires: Desires for accomplishment, recognition, and success
- Emotional desires: The desire to give and receive love; desires for compassion, forgiveness, and peace
- Self-expression desires: The desire to speak your truth, to be heard and understood
- Insight desires: To know your higher self, to know truth; to transcend
- Unification desires: To merge and become one with all things; to experience enlightenment

Ask yourself what you want on a regular basis. Become aware of your desires and intentions. Write them down (see the Law of Intention and Desire) and keep them privately tucked away within your awareness. As your desires become fulfilled, new intentions will take their place, naturally leading you to a better understanding of yourself and what you have come here to do.

What Is My Purpose?
The third question invites us to explore the reason for our presence in this lifetime. With the expanded perspective gained through the first two questions, we begin to have glimpses of the reason(s) we are here. The answer to this question may change and evolve as you continue to explore its depths. For example, you might consider your purpose:

- To have a family
- To have a job
- To work
- To teach
- To heal
- To create
- To grow and evolve
- To know my higher self
- To love and be loved
- To be happy
- To serve
- To be

Notice that with each answer, the purpose moves from *having*, to *doing*, to *being*. As our purpose becomes increasingly refined, we identify less with our ego, and more with our spirit. The voice of the ego asks, "What's in it for me?" while the voice of spirit asks, "How can I serve, and how can I help?" This question continues to shift your internal reference point from local to non-local, from self to other, from individual to universal.

In the Buddhist tradition, the fifth step on the Noble Eightfold Path to Enlightenment is *right livelihood*. This principle is about aligning your values, your vocation, and your purpose into a unified synthesis that tractor beams your life in the direction it was meant to go. Every experience in your life has been preparing you for the person you are meant to be and what you are meant to do. As you continue to ask yourself what your purpose is, your life's calling will unmask itself for you.

What Am I Grateful For?

This final question helps us to put our attention on those things we have to be thankful for in our lives. It is the keystone of a gratitude practice in which we shift out of the conventional mindset of lack and into a state of wealth or abundance consciousness. Putting our attention on those things, people, or situations that fill our hearts with gratitude and appreciation does two powerful things.

First, thinking grateful thoughts leads to actual *feelings* of gratitude. This emotion of gratitude not only feels good, but has a corresponding biochemical state that has a powerful effect on our health. As we cultivate gratitude, we:

- Lower our stress levels
- Reduce inflammation
- Lower the risk of depression
- Lower our blood pressure
- Improve our sleep patterns

Second, as we regularly put our attention on what we have and what we're grateful for, we create the mental habit of looking for more things to be grateful for. Consistently taking in the good *makes it easier to see more good in the world*, helping to essentially overwrite the brain's negativity bias and appreciate life for the miracle it is.

> *When you realize there is nothing lacking,*
> *the whole world belongs to you.*
>
> —Lao Tzu

Now that we've explored these profound life questions, how do you use them to enhance your meditation practice? It's simple. Once you've prepared yourself to meditate (and perhaps practiced one of the breathing exercises from the previous section), close your eyes and allow yourself to settle and relax. Now softly place your attention in the area of your heart. Notice your heartbeat, and in that stillness, silently repeat the first question: Who am I? Don't look for an answer or struggle to make something happen. Simply let the question echo throughout your consciousness. Be with the question, feeling free to gently repeat it one or two more times for about a minute. Then proceed to the second question: What do I want? Follow the same procedure for the remaining two questions.

Once you complete the fourth question, simply let go of all the questions along with any answers or images that may have come to mind. Release them completely and allow yourself to be free from any expectations. See this as an opportunity to open the dialogue between your local and non-local selves. Having opened the door to your soul, you can now begin the repetition of the mantra knowing that the questions will stir the field of infinite possibilities and bring you the answers and insights you need at the most appropriate time.

SO-HUM REVISITED

If you recall from Chapter 1 when I introduced you to the so-hum mantra I explained that the mantra is used for its vibrational quality rather than for a particular meaning. While this is accurate as it relates to the English language, I would like to take a deeper dive into the theory and understanding of the so-hum mantra as described by the Vedic and Yogic philosophy. In so doing we will discover the subtle qualities of this powerful technique and add another layer to your practice.

First, know that the so-hum practice is an ancient, time-tested meditation technique. It has been used for thousands of years and has its roots firmly established in the Vedic literature, specifically in the Isha Upanishad. The mantra consists of two Sanskrit words, *so* and *hum*. So means "that" and hum means "I." In this context, "that" refers to infinite, unbounded, universal pure consciousness. "That" may seem like an odd usage of an impersonal pronoun; however, it is a convenient way to encapsulate the notion that everything outside of you is a mirror of the ultimate reality. The "I" is the individual ego self or "myself." It represents our constricted, conditioned, and narrow object-referred identity. Put together, these words mean, "I am that" or "I am one with the universe." Therefore, the so-hum mantra signifies a unification of the smaller self with the higher self—the merging of the individual with the universal.

So-hum is also considered to be the mantra of the breath and is one of the most frequently used mantra pranayama techniques. If you listen closely to the cycle of your breath, you will be able to hear the soft sound of "so" on the inhale and "hum" on the exhale. Through the gentle repetition of the mantra we amplify this primordial sound in our consciousness and harness its subtly powerful vibration.

At this point it's worth mentioning the unique relationship between sound and meaning as it relates to the Sanskrit language. Sanskrit, the language of ancient India, is a fascinating component of Vedanta and the yogic philosophy. Considered by many scholars to be the *mother of tongues*, Sanskrit is unlike most of the familiar Indo-European languages that are based primarily on meaning alone. Sanskrit is based upon both the *meaning* and *the sound or vibration* of the words spoken. For example, we know that the English word "abundance" means to have plenty or to be prosperous. But compare that to the Sanskrit seed mantra *shrim* (pronounced *shreem*). This word not only represents the principle of abundance in all its forms, but it is also the *vibration* of abundance. Therefore, repeating or chanting this mantra causes your mind and body to resonate with the vibration of abundance, rather than it just being an intellectual understanding.

When you say or mentally repeat a mantra you are generating a specific vibration in your subtle and physical body that ripples throughout your entire being. As you repeat so-hum, you're not simply affirming that you are one with the universe or the ultimate reality; you're creating a vibrational and energetic effect that tunes your frequency to that of infinite consciousness. In this way mantras are like yoga poses for the mind; they hold our attention in a specific position, liberate us from blockages, dissolve rigidity, and build mental energy, balance, flexibility, and strength.

In addition, according to Vedanta, when we use powerful and traditional mantras (such as so-hum) we tap into the collective stream of spiritual energy that has been cultivated by millions of meditators over thousands of years. Potent, well-used mantras may generate what scientist Rupert Sheldrake, PhD, calls *morphic resonance* or "a process whereby self-organizing systems inherit a memory from previous similar systems." In other words, the more frequently a mantra has been used, the stronger its effect will be, and the more likely it will have a similar outcome.

Thus we can see the so-hum mantra in a much deeper context. It is a simple and elegant technique, one that requires no special training or initiation and can be practiced by anyone, yet it can be a profound tool for shifting your identity from local to non-local. It creates a powerful and healing vibration in the mind and body. It serves as a bridge reaching far into the past, connecting you to the rich history and spiritual inheritance of ancient seers and sages who have walked this path before us. Most importantly, it is an ever-present reminder of who you are—the one who knows deep within: I am that.

OTHER MANTRAS

Although the practice I've explained in this book is centered around the so-hum mantra, it is one of literally thousands of mantras in the Vedic and Yogic teachings alone; not to mention mantras from other traditions. The purpose in using the so-hum mantra is that it is a universal mantra that can be used by anyone and is a tried-and-true mantra to establish your practice. However, if you are interested in taking your practice deeper by exploring other mantras, I wanted to share some of them here. Know that for each of the mantras explained below, the practice would be the same as with the so-hum mantra, but with two exceptions:

1. Where the so-hum mantra is meant to flow with the breath, these mantras are meant to be repeated independent of your breath. Simply repeat them effortlessly and innocently and allow the vibration of the mantra to take you into expanded states of consciousness.
2. These mantras don't need to be confined to a formal seated meditation practice. You can repeat these mantras during your daily activity, such as while walking, eating, or performing household tasks. Of course, your eyes would be open and you would be paying attention to your surroundings while repeating the mantra. Nevertheless, you will discover that using a mantra during activity is an effective way to help focus and settle a restless internal dialogue.

Also, as several of these additional mantras are in Sanskrit, remember the vibrational nature of Sanskrit and recognize that although they have an approximate English translation, the sound quality of the mantra is of primary importance. While there is a meaning associated with these mantras, you don't need to hard-focus or concentrate on it. Simply let the sound wash over you and detach from the outcome. Explore each of the mantras and see if one or several resonate with you personally.

Om (OHM)

Om is the most well-known of all Sanskrit mantras. It has been used for thousands of years as well as made its way into popular culture. I've lost track of how many times, when mentioning meditation to someone, that even with no knowledge or experience, they will close their eyes and jokingly chant a pronounced "ommmm." However, in reality, om has a specific and powerful meaning. It is considered to be the "hymn of the universe," or the vibration of the entire cosmos. It contains, and is the source, of all sounds and all vibrations.

Om actually is three sounds in one, AH, OH, and M. In Vedanta, yoga, and Hinduism, om represents the trinity of existence—creation, the sound of AH; preservation, the sound OH; and destruction, the M sound. Om is the sound of the seventh *chakra* or psycho-physiological energy center of the body at which your personal soul merges into the universal soul. Om may be used singularly on its own as a mantra to calm the mind and reconnect to your true essence. It is also often used at the beginning of other Sanskrit mantras as a means to energize and supercharge the mantras that follow it.

Ram (RAHM)

In Sanskrit, ram is one of the multiple names for God. Ram is a classic mantra in the Hindu tradition and is said to cultivate joy in the mind and heart. It is also the mantra of the third chakra, which is associated with your desires, intentions, and will.

Om Mani Padme Hum (OM MAH-NEE PAHD-MEY HOOM)

This mantra is part of the Buddhist tradition and has been used by seekers for centuries. It means "the jewel in the lotus of the heart." It refers to the spark of divine consciousness hidden within each of us. This mantra is also known as the mantra of the Bodhisattvas—highly evolved spiritual beings who, rather than continue their growth to the final stage of enlightenment, choose to remain in the physical domain for the sake of sentient beings everywhere. It is a mantra of compassion for all beings on the path to unity consciousness.

Om Namah Sivaya (OM NAH-MAH SHEE VAH YAH)
Om namah sivaya is the great Shiva mantra. In the Vedic tradition, Shiva was the first yogi and the source of all yogic knowledge. Shiva was also known as the *great destroyer*; however, Shiva represents the destruction of ignorance and negative tendencies that obstruct our personal growth. This is the mantra of the *Siddha* or perfected being; one who has transformed their own darkness into light.

Aham Brahmasmi (AH-HUM BRAH-MAHS-MEE)
This mantra is one of the *Mahavakyas*—the great or profound sayings of Vedanta. These sayings are concentrated packets of information that are meant to bring about a transformation in consciousness. Aham Brahmasmi means, "I am the universe; I am pure, divine consciousness." This mantra is a reminder of your true identity—a unique focal point of awareness in an infinite universe of consciousness.

Om Gum Ganapatayei Namaha (OM GUM GUH-NUH-PUT-YEI NAHM-AH-HA)
This classic mantra is the mantra of Lord Ganesha, the Hindu deity of wisdom and the remover of obstacles. Using this mantra is said to help remove inner and outer barriers to success, happiness, and fulfillment. As such, this mantra is also often used for healing and the removal of energy blockages within the body.

Om Shanti Om (OM SHAHN-TEE OM)
Shanti means "peace" in Sanskrit, so this is a mantra for individual, collective, and universal peace. It creates a peaceful vibration within that resonates into the local environment and the world.

Sa Ta Na Ma (SAH TAH NAH MAH)
This Kundalini yoga mantra encapsulates the eternal circle of life: birth, life, death, and rebirth. Sa means "birth," ta means "life," na is "death," and ma is "rebirth." This mantra helps to prepare the mind and body for transformation and is also a reminder of our true identity as consciousness in a never-ending state of transformation. It is known for its uplifting effect and can be sung, whispered, or repeated silently.

Wahe Guru (WAH-HAY GU-ROO)
Another Kundalini yoga mantra, Wahe Guru, is the mantra of ecstasy. It is the ecstasy of spiritual bliss experienced as we go from ignorance to enlightenment. *Wahe* means "wonderful," and *guru* means "teacher" or "remover of darkness." This mantra is chanted aloud or repeated silently to express the joy of awakening or to summon divine light to remove our ignorance.

Shalom (SHAH-LOHM)
The Hebrew word *shalom* is commonly translated as "peace;" however, it comes from a root word meaning "wholeness." This wholeness is meant to represent the joining together of opposites or the unifying of all layers and experiences of life. To be peaceful, we must be whole. Using shalom as a mantra embodies the peace we feel when we see the other in ourselves and ourselves in the other.

Be Still and Know that I Am God
This often-quoted biblical passage is from Psalm 46:10. I've included it as an additional mantra because I feel it embodies the deeper understanding of meditation practice. When we meditate, we are "being still." Our bodies and minds are settled, and on occasion we go into the gap of deepest stillness and glimpse our soul, our divine true nature. We make direct and intimate contact with the non-local, infinite, immeasurable, eternal, field of all that was, is, or ever will be. For some, that

field is the universe, for others, it is God. Ultimately, God is everything and everywhere, including you yourself.

The Lord Is My Shepherd
This well-known and beloved Christian mantra comes from Psalm 23. It symbolizes the protective power of Christ and serves as a reminder that he is looking out for us and will come to our aid. In secular language, the shepherd is an archetype that represents one who guides, teaches, leads, and protects those who are less capable. This is a helpful mantra in times of trouble but is also a mantra of trust in powers greater than ourselves to deliver us from harm.

Thy Will Be Done
This mantra is the third petition of the Lord's Prayer in the Christian faith. It is a mantra of surrender; a conscious and deliberate affirmation of letting go of our attachment to an outcome. This mantra powerfully embodies the Law of Detachment and allows us to stop playing general manager of the universe. In repeating "Thy Will Be Done," we are turning our challenges, our struggles, our intentions, and our desires over to cosmic intelligence. There's a joke that goes, "If you want to make God laugh, tell him *your* plans." This mantra is yielding to the infinite mind of the universe and trusting that its plans for your life are better than you could ever imagine.

THE HEART SUTRAS
Another powerful enhancement to your meditation practice is the heart sutras. The Sanskrit word *sutra* means "discourse;" it's a concise verse or scripture that has a potent, consciousness-shifting effect. Sutra also means "thread" or "to stitch together." Sutras are strands of intention between the local and non-local levels of consciousness. Like tethers that lead us back to our true selves, sutras can trigger transformations

in our awareness and awaken what the sage Patanjali called *dormant potentialities*.

The heart sutras, as the name suggests, involves activating the heart's subtle energy center or *chakra* through the repetition of four sutras (words). Each of the sutras are meant to be embedded into our consciousness when we are settled and silent, immediately following a period of meditation. In this way they are "planted" deep within where they can take root, having the most powerful and transformative effect. Here's how to integrate the heart sutras into your meditation practice.

- Practice the so-hum meditation as normal. Upon the completion of your mantra meditation, simply be in the stillness for a few moments.
- Now move your awareness to the area of your heart. Notice the sensations there. See if you can feel your heart beating or the warmth of your circulation.
- Still keeping your attention in your heart, imagine or visualize a beautiful still pond or a tranquil mountain lake—free from any disturbance, quiet, calm, and perfectly settled.
- Now silently repeat the following words four times each, pausing for about fifteen seconds after each repetition: peace . . . harmony . . . laughter . . . love.
- With each sutra, imagine a small pebble dropping into the water, creating ripples that spread out from your heart center, passing throughout your mind and body, and continuing out into the *entire universe*.
- Upon completing the sutras, sit quietly and imagine the ripples settling back into stillness and silence before moving back into activity.

You may also repeat the sutras without the visualization; I find it to be a pleasing way to imagine the way our intentions radiate out into the field of consciousness. If you choose not to use the imagery, simply keep your awareness in your heart as you release each sutra every fifteen seconds.

In practicing the heart sutras regularly, you will begin to embody those qualities from the deepest level of your being. You will start to align your personal vibrational field with that of universal peace, harmony, laughter, and love so that the words aren't merely sentimental ideas; they are the truth at the core of your being.

THE METTA PRAYER

The metta prayer is a foundational Buddhist meditation practice designed to cultivate compassion toward self, others, and the entire universe. The word *metta* comes from the Pali language, the language spoken at the time of the historical Buddha. It means "lovingkindness" or "good will." It is an intentional prayer of kindness that progressively expands your awareness from your localized seat of self-awareness, to your local group of friends, family, and acquaintances, out further to your nearby community, on to the global community, and ultimately the entire universe.

The metta prayer is a powerful way to "uncouple" ourselves from our normal ego-centric awareness so that we may embrace others in lovingkindness that they, too, may be happy and free from suffering. In regular practice, it cultivates unconditional love, compassion, forgiveness, and understanding. In an esoteric sense, it is like giving the whole world a big hug. It embraces all of humanity and all living beings in a field of love and acceptance. Similar to the heart sutras, the metta prayer is a powerful intention that broadcasts healing blessings to all of existence and, as we've seen, intentions are transformational forces of nature. Use the metta prayer regularly to project a wave of compassion into the world.

What follows is a basic version of the metta prayer that you can merge into your existing practice. As with the heart sutras, upon completion of your mantra practice, be still and allow the stillness and silence to wash over you. After a minute or two, begin to silently repeat (or read) the metta prayer to yourself. Repeat each line slowly and deliberately, allowing an image to form in your mind. At the end of the prayer, remain in silence for a few minutes, embracing the compassion and lovingkindness you have just generated for yourself and the world.

May I live in happiness
May I be safe from inner and outer danger
May I be healthy in mind and body
May I live my life with ease

May (a close friend or family member) live in happiness
May (a close friend or family member) be safe from inner and outer danger
May (a close friend or family member) be healthy in mind and body
May (a close friend or family member) live their life (or lives) with ease

May my perceived enemies live in happiness
May my perceived enemies be safe from inner and outer danger
May my perceived enemies be healthy in mind and body
May my perceived enemies live their life (or lives) with ease

May (a community, city, or location) live in happiness
May (a community, city, or location) be safe from inner and outer danger
May (a community, city, or location) be healthy in mind and body
May (a community, city, or location) live their life (or lives) with ease

May the world live in happiness
May the world be safe from inner and outer danger
May the world be healthy in mind and body
May all creation realize its own Divine nature

May we all live our lives with ease
May we all gain enlightenment for the benefit of all beings

TONGLEN PRACTICE

Tonglen is a Tibetan Buddhist meditation technique that also focuses on generating compassion. Tonglen means "giving and taking." In this practice we take in and absorb the pain or suffering of others and give back compassion, peace, and love. Like a spiritual vacuum cleaner, we draw in the dark, murky clouds of despair, negativity, anger, or other forms of misery that are afflicting others and then, like a radiant sun, we shine forth light, clarity, understanding, and whatever other attributes will benefit them.

Now you might be saying, "I've got enough of my own negativity to manage, I don't think I can handle taking on the suffering of another." Or maybe you're worried that through this practice you'll somehow contaminate your own energetic field and let the pain of another create a "spiritual drag" on your life force. I want you to remember two things. First, the clarity of your intention during this practice sets up the preconditions for your experience. Having a focused intention to draw in negativity and emit positivity back out into the world will help to spontaneously bring about the desired effect. Second, the *real you*, as we've discussed previously, is a field of unbounded, infinite, *absolutely pure consciousness*. And when I say pure, I mean untaintable, unblemishable, and invulnerable to all insults or pollutants. Nothing can put even the slightest dent in the immaculate purity of that field of awareness. As Krishna describes the field of consciousness to Arjuna in the *Bhagavad Gita* Chapter 2, Verse 23-24: *The self cannot be pierced by weapons or burned by fire; water cannot wet it, nor the wind dry it. The Self cannot be pierced or burned, made wet or dry. It is everlasting and infinite, standing on the motionless foundations of eternity.*

TAKING YOUR PRACTICE DEEPER

So know that when you perform Tonglen, you are acting as the funnel for some of the world's hurt. But as it is exposed to the field of pure awareness, it is transformed and dissolved entirely, allowing you to project the qualities of spirit back into the world.

To practice the Tonglen technique, follow these steps:

- Spend seven to ten minutes performing the so-hum meditation. Give yourself at least this much time to settle your awareness and make contact with the stillness at the core of your being.
- Stop repeating the so-hum mantra and let the silence sink in. Visualize yourself as an extension of the field of pure consciousness, a node in the vast web of universal awareness—infinite, unbounded, and invincible.
- Next, put your attention on a person, situation, or relationship that needs healing. Have the intention to transmute the negativity into a higher state of consciousness.
- Now as you inhale, imagine or visualize that you are breathing in a thick smog—a dark, cold, heavy cloud of negativity and suffering. Imagine it being sucked out of the space and drawn into your body. Take in only as much as feels comfortable for you.
- Pause just briefly enough to imagine the cloud of pain contained within you being pierced by a spark of brilliant light in the center of your chest. Like a light-speed supernova explosion, watch the spark burst out into a shockwave of blue-white light that instantaneously vaporizes the cloud of negativity.
- Exhale, radiating out an expanding bubble of light, compassion, healing, peace, and love. Allow the bubble to fill up the space, permeating every nook and cranny down to the smallest speck of dust. See the healing light embrace anyone in the area, cleansing them of their pain and hurt.

- Repeat the process with each breath, taking in negativity, and radiating compassion to whatever degree feels appropriate for you. Continue for as long as it feels comfortable to do so.
- On your final exhalation of this process, see the bubble of light and love expanding out beyond the limits of time and space and into the entire universe.
- Sit comfortably in the stillness before returning to your regular activity.

You can use this practice in a localized area, projected on others that may not be with you physically, or even into the past to help bring healing and transformation.

A SAMPLE ROUTINE

In this chapter I've outlined quite a few tools to help you take your meditation practice deeper. However, you may be wondering how to fit them into your personal routine. To give you an example, here's how I integrate several of these add-ons into my personal meditation practice.

As I settle in and get ready to meditate, I take a moment or two to reflect on one of the Seven Spiritual Laws of Success. Doing this helps put my attention on the background theme of my day. Once I'm seated comfortably, I'll usually perform a few rounds of one of the breathing exercises. For my morning meditation I almost always use the bellows breath because it helps wake me up and energize my system after sleeping. In the evening, my go-to exercises are usually balanced breathing or the success breath. These help me de-frag and let go of any stress that's been hanging on from the day.

Next, I'll take perhaps two minutes to ask myself the four big questions of: Who am I? What do I want? What is my purpose? What am I grateful for? I don't necessarily go looking for answers; I just let them echo off the canyons of my mind and see where they lead.

TAKING YOUR PRACTICE DEEPER

At this point, I settle into my standard mantra practice. Typically, I set an app timer for either twenty-four or twenty-one minutes; twenty-four because that equals one minute of meditation for each hour of the day, and twenty-one just because I've always liked it. Either way, as often as time allows, I aim for at least twenty minutes repeating the mantra.

Once I've completed my mantra practice, I'll sit in silence for a few moments, after which I'll do the heart sutras at least two times each. This usually concludes my regular meditation practice. However, in times of challenge or frustration, I will often add on a metta prayer or Tonglen technique to help ease the suffering of the world in whatever way I can.

It's important to note that these add-ons, just like everything we've discussed in this book, should be used in a way that is comfortable for you. Experiment, mix and match, or just stick with the reliable standard so-hum. Don't feel the need to become a meditation Olympic-level athlete if that's not your thing. It's far better to incorporate one additional element to a regular consistent practice than try to load up on too many extra bells and whistles and eventually lose interest. These tools are all meant to help enhance your practice, not bog it down or make it a chore. Start out small; as time goes on see if your interest in new practices grows. And remember, have fun with it!

CHAPTER 10

MEDITATION TO SHAPE NEW BELIEFS

Over the years, either through my personal study and explorations in human potential and self-improvement, or as a byproduct of my meditation practice, I have become exceptionally fascinated by *beliefs*. In particular, understanding what beliefs are, where they come from, why we believe what we do, and how we can change limiting beliefs into more empowering ones. Beliefs form a foundational component of our sense of self; therefore, examining them objectively helps us to know ourselves better. As it turns out, meditation is an ideal tool to not only explore what and why we believe what we do, but also a way to transform or transcend beliefs that constrict or limit our awareness.

WHAT IS A BELIEF?

A *belief* is an idea, notion, or strong opinion of something that we accept and consider to be true. It's a state of mind in which we think something is a reality either with or without empirical evidence to support it. Beliefs are convictions and assumptions about the way the world is, how it works, and what it all means. Each of us are a collection of beliefs, an assembled network of ideas, opinions, perspectives, and attitudes that we hold on countless subjects. We have ideological beliefs, religious beliefs, political and moral beliefs, beliefs about cultural issues, and beliefs about who we are and what we're ultimately capable of. These beliefs influence our perceptions, govern our attitudes, and filter our worldview.

Generally speaking, there are two types of beliefs: constricted and limiting, or expansive and evolutionary. As you might guess, constricted beliefs confine and trap awareness into a narrow and stagnant mental construct, leading to entropy and regression. On the other hand, expansive beliefs open the door to growth, freedom, unbounded energy, and the forward pull of unlimited possibilities. Since we are a reflection of the collected beliefs we hold, we have the ability to consciously choose beliefs that will define who we are. As a sculptor molds clay, our beliefs shape who we will become. It is, therefore, in our best interest to choose beliefs that are expansive, inspiring, positive, and uplifting. In this way our beliefs become a template that guides our thoughts, speech, and actions toward a life of happiness, joy, and fulfillment.

Let me give you an example of how beliefs can condition our thoughts and behavior. Flashback to 1985–86. I was in high school—unsure of what I wanted to do with my life after I graduated. I didn't have any firm plans, and even though I had interviewed at several colleges, I wasn't feeling it—no doubt to my parent's chagrin.

However, for a brief period I became infatuated with the idea of joining the Navy. Flashback to my flashback—one of the first movies I ever saw, and still to this day one of my favorites, was Walt Disney's *20,000 Leagues Under the Sea*. I loved the idea of submarines and as a kid I often thought about how cool it would be to have my own *Nautilus* in which I could cruise around the waterways of Western Pennsylvania.

Anyway, at some point while researching colleges, I discovered that one of the universities I was considering had a Navy ROTC program. My reasoning went something like this: College leads to ROTC, ROTC leads to becoming naval officer, and being a naval officer meant I would be a submariner. I know, it probably sounds silly, but as a high school kid it seemed like a good idea at the time and it gave me something to aim for, even if it wasn't the most well thought out plan. I wanted to be a sub driver, so why not?

However, when I rather excitedly told my girlfriend that I wanted to join the Navy to be on a submarine, the conversation went something like this:

"You're too tall to be on a submarine."

"I am?"

"Yeah, they have height restrictions and you're too tall."

"Oh."

The belief that I was too tall to be on a submarine had been planted and in a flash it grew, reprogramming within me what was possible. In case you're wondering, I wasn't too tall to be on a submarine. I'm 6 feet tall and the submarine height limit is 6'4". But it didn't matter; I believed I was too tall, and I believed it so well I didn't even think to check for myself. I saw my girlfriend as an authority (possibly because she was older than me), took her word as gospel, and without question assumed it to be true.

I share this as an object lesson of how beliefs influence our thoughts and actions, and define what we believe is possible. Would I have become a submarine commander had I not believed I was too tall? Would I be living a completely different life had I not been influenced by that single belief? Who knows. The point I'm making is that beliefs have the power to change the course of a life. Therefore, it's our duty to know what and why we believe what we do, to validate our beliefs with empirical evidence, and make sure we haven't become trapped by false or limiting information.

> *Can you remember who you were, before the world told you who you should be?*
>
> —Charles Burkowski

WHERE DO BELIEFS COME FROM?

Where do we get our beliefs? We'd all like to think that our beliefs are consciously, rationally arrived at through a process of well-informed critical thinking; however, in reality it's not so simple. The formation of a belief is less of something that we actively do, and much more something that *happens to us*. To a large extent, our beliefs are the product of inherited programming we received as children from our environment. When I say environment, I'm referring to our younger selves' primary sources of knowledge—parents, siblings, teachers, religious leaders, peers, the media, and anyone we consider an authority figure.

In his amazing book, *The Biology of Belief*, author and cell biologist Bruce Lipton describes the new science of *epigenetics*, which studies the biological and perceptual mechanisms that turn genes on and off.[1] Lipton explains that children between the ages of two and six are in an early stage of brain development that makes them extremely receptive to absorbing new information. If you remember the discussion on brainwave activity from Chapter 4, you may recall how the theta brainwave frequency of 4–8 Hz created a relaxed and expansive state of awareness. This is the brainwave state in which we all lived out our early childhood, essentially in a perpetual download mode—highly suggestible and open to all types of new information. This information is sponged up by the subconscious mind without going through any filters, critical thought, or tests for accuracy. At this early stage, a child's brain simply hasn't developed the neural structures to reason and think through the incoming data, let alone question the authority of where the information is coming from. In this way, concepts, moral values, beliefs, worldviews, and ideologies are mapped into a child's developing brain, with little if any choice on their part.

It's as if beliefs are software programs installed on a new computer. The programs could be highly rated and well developed or they could be garbage. The computer doesn't know the difference; it just runs the program that's been installed. The program may also affect other

MEDITATION TO SHAPE NEW BELIEFS

programs running in the background, subtly influencing the computer's performance. As time goes on, the software becomes increasingly woven into the computer's operation making it difficult to fix or uninstall the program.

Beliefs are formed in much the same way that concrete is poured for a building's foundation. As the cement is laid down, it is fluid and malleable, but within a few hours it begins to harden, and after a day or so it has become fixed, rigid, and rock-solid. Similarly, beliefs become "set" and reinforce themselves through a process known as *confirmation bias*. This is the tendency to only seek out information or evidence that supports a particular viewpoint or belief. Rather than look for the truth independent of any preconceived notions, our confirmation bias compels us to data mine or cherry-pick information that fits in with what we already believe. It's for this reason that we often find ourselves becoming increasingly set in our ways as we grow older. By relying on confirmation bias to only seek out more reasons to believe what do, our worldview becomes a self-sustaining feedback loop.

Now this is all well and good if the beliefs you hold are nourishing and life affirming. But what do you do if your beliefs are narrow, constricting, or negatively affecting your well-being? This is where the transformative power of meditation comes in. In fact, meditation is possibly *the most effective* way to revise and shape new beliefs. Here's how it works.

First, through meditation we create the space to *hold* our beliefs. The stillness of meditation becomes a vessel within which we can contain our beliefs, witness them, and accept them for what they are. The observer or space consciousness is free from judgment and allows you to be fully aware of what you believe and why you believe it. This is a process of discovering the causes of our own ignorance. Although it can be uncomfortable at times, we must first recognize and accept our beliefs before we can hope to change them.

Additionally, by owning and understanding our beliefs, we begin to see how they are unconsciously activated by a particular stimulus. This knowledge in and of itself is incredibly liberating because it gives us the opportunity to make conscious choices and respond with awareness rather than getting caught up in a repetitive cycle of habitual reactivity.

Meditation further allows us to *see through our own self-deception*. While none of us like to admit it, we fool ourselves all the time. Whether through confirmation biases or other logical fallacies, we routinely find ways to defend our beliefs to our own personal ends. Even when they run up against a mountain of evidence to the contrary, we will often stubbornly dig in our heels to defend our views rather than consider that our beliefs are faulty or in error. We do this through a process called *cognitive dissonance*. Cognitive dissonance is the uncomfortable feeling we have whenever we hold two or more contradictory beliefs. For example, whenever you hold a particular belief that goes against an enormous amount of evidence that refutes your position, you will feel mental discomfort and stress due to these dual beliefs struggling for dominance in your consciousness. Whenever you experience cognitive dissonance, you have a choice—either 1) reconsider or modify your beliefs on that subject or 2) double down and pretend the conflicting position doesn't exist.

The beauty of meditation is that by fostering increased mental clarity and intellectual honestly it helps us see through our own nonsense. We become more adept at spotting our own biases and predispositions to follow a particular self-serving narrative. The truth is, the more you practice meditation, the more difficult it becomes to hide the truth from yourself.

> *Becoming "awake" involves seeing our confusion more clearly.*
>
> —Chogyam Trungpa

An allegory that helps to expand this understanding is the classic teaching of mistaking a rope for a snake. Walking down a road in poor lighting, we might easily believe that a coiled rope is a snake blocking our path. However, if we have a flashlight, we will discover that what we thought was a potentially dangerous animal was nothing of the kind. We may in fact laugh at ourselves for not having seen it for what is was. In the same way, the lucidity cultivated through meditation practice helps us see things (including our deeply cherished beliefs) *as they are*, rather than as we think or want them to be.

Next, meditation helps us to *transcend* our limiting beliefs. When we meditate, we go beyond our conscious thoughts as well as our subconscious beliefs. All the outworn, outdated, and stale beliefs that we've carried since childhood are temporarily bypassed as we expand our awareness. The more regularly we do this, the less they are able to influence our thoughts, speech, and behavior. Every time we transcend, we step outside of the constricting shackles of restrictive beliefs. Our subconscious programming becomes less dominant and where we once may have felt the need to rigidly defend our beliefs and opinions, we now feel the birth of defenselessness in our awareness.

Meditation also awakens within us the more expansive *unconditioned mind*. When you get down to it, all beliefs (even the supportive ones) are *conditions*; they are restrictions we place on our reality. They are ways we chop up the infinite oneness of the universe into manageable thought-pieces. However, when we meditate, we return to a state beyond conditions. For a few precious moments each day, all those divisions, limits, and beliefs dissolve back into a field of unity. The great thing about this is that it reminds us that our beliefs aren't fixed or permanent. They don't exist without us to believe them; they are impermanent mental constructs that have a beginning, a middle, and an end.

Additionally, meditation is the great *purifier of consciousness*. Each time we go into the gap between our thoughts, we enter a realm of immaculate purity that is immune to all forms of contamination. Any negativity, hostility, fear, doubt, or otherwise limiting beliefs are dissolved in the light and awareness of the unified field. The conditional mind state that is so familiar in our day-to-day lives falls away during meditation allowing us to merge back into the ocean of spirit. Like skins of an onion being gently peeled away, our old, outdated beliefs fall off, one by one, revealing our truest, highest self—an unconditioned soul swimming in a vast sea of awareness.

Finally, through meditation, we experience *true liberation* or *moksha*. Moksha means "ultimate freedom and liberation" in Sanskrit. This is not freedom in the ordinary sense. For many of us when we hear or think the word "freedom" we associate it with a nationalistic ideal—the freedom of speech, to bear arms, to come and go as we please, or "life, liberty, and the pursuit of happiness." However, these things aren't true or ultimate freedoms; they are conditional symbols—impermanent concepts that we use to placate ourselves into believing we are actually free. Moksha goes much deeper; it is the release from the limitations of our conventional worldly existence.

Whether we are aware of it or not, we are all prisoners of the intellect. We are trapped by limiting ideas we have built up around ourselves over the course of a lifetime. It is with this conditional thinking that we have defined ourselves—what we can do, what we can't; our so-called strengths and weaknesses; our skills and talents; our sense of self-worth and value—all of these live rent-free in our minds. As long as we are imprisoned by our conditioning, no amount of external liberties will give us true freedom. True freedom only arises when we can step outside of the boundaries and roles we have used to constrict our awareness. Those boundaries are built from the habits and patterns we have layered upon ourselves since we were children.

Here again is the blessing of meditation. Interrupting the mind-stream that carries the thoughts, concepts, and definitions inherent in our consciousness causes our conditional identity and belief network to loosen its grasp on us. The more time we spend in unbounded, unconditional awareness, the more it begins to feel like our true home. Unconditional acceptance begins to permeate our being and becomes our ground state during daily activity. Beliefs, patterns, and habitual thinking are still present, but they no longer have control over us. We can witness those mental constructs and make conscious choices toward more expansive states of awareness. *True freedom* is freedom from the past, freedom from the person we used to be, and freedom from the rules and conditional life that once dominated our awareness. This is moksha, ultimate liberation, peace, and oneness with the absolute.

Ultimately, through the practice of meditation, we are able to make the shift from belief to *knowing*. We make conscious contact with the truth at the core of our being, tap into the deepest level of reality, and access knowledge and understanding through direct experience. Beliefs are based upon conceptual mental constructs; knowing comes from a tangible, personal communion with that understanding. Bruce Lee used to refer to this concept as "dry land swimming," meaning that no amount of talking or theorizing about swimming will ever convey the reality of jumping in the water and doing it.

Meditation opens the door to our direct experience of who we are, what we are capable of, and the possibilities that lie within. It is the gateway to living a life beyond limits.

CHAPTER 11

AN END TO SUFFERING

> *As long as you think that the cause of your problem is "out there"—as long as you think that anyone or anything is responsible for your suffering—the situation is hopeless. It means that you are forever in the role of victim, that you're suffering in paradise.*
>
> —Byron Katie

The first of the Buddha's Four Noble Truths can be stated simply: Life contains suffering. None of us will argue this fact. The human condition contains ups, downs, joys, sorrows, pleasures, pains, and *suffering*. What sets suffering apart from pain, however, is that when we suffer, we identify with our pain as being an aspect of our being. It's an interpretation of a painful situation that we take personally—a state of distress and hardship that we undergo and feel victimized by. Pain is an uncomfortable physical, mental, or emotional experience. Suffering is resistance to the pain, the "woe is me" or "it's not fair; I shouldn't be going through this" experience that magnifies the pain through anxiety, denial, and anger. In life, pain is inevitable; suffering, however, is optional.

According to Vedanta, understanding suffering is the key to freedom from it. Meditation is a fundamental part of this process, which is why I've chosen to explore it in its own chapter. Let's take a closer look at these teachings to learn how meditation can serve as a vehicle for Moksha, or liberation from suffering.

In Chapter 2 of the *Yoga Sutras of Patanjali*, we are introduced to the five causes of suffering. These are known as the *five kleshas*. The Sanskrit word klesha means "poison" or those conditions and obstacles that prevent us from clear perception and lead to suffering. The five kleshas are:

1. **Not knowing the true nature of reality.** Known as *avidya* in Sanskrit, this klesha refers to the state of delusion or incorrect understanding that obscures reality behind the veil of materialism. It is the deep state of "not knowing," yet it in no way implies failure or wrongdoing on our part. Rather, we simply don't know what we don't know. Daily life in our material-based existence coupled with the turbulent activity of our minds washes out awareness of the deeper layers of reality, keeping it hidden from view.

    What then is the true nature of reality? According to the world's greatest wisdom traditions, the world—the universe—is an eternal, unbounded, infinite field of consciousness or pure awareness. As Carl Sagan described it in his book *Cosmos* and the award-winning television series of the same name, "The Cosmos is all that is or ever was or ever will be." Known in Vedanta as *brahman*, the true nature of the world is a field of indestructible, supreme, and absolute pure spirit. It is the omnipresent, omniscient, omnipotent self of everything, giving rise to all forms and phenomena. Without beginning or ending, there is nowhere it isn't; it is the Self of all things.

    When we don't know the true nature of reality as brahman or pure consciousness, we get caught up or lost in the illusions of material reality. We fail to realize that the world of hard stuff, things, buildings, cars, bodies, countries, planets, and galaxies are simply the shadows of a much deeper level of reality. We mistake the map for the territory and fool ourselves into accepting that the mirage is real. It's as if we are looking at the world through a dirty window. Until we clean the dirt off, we'll always have a mistaken and skewed view of the world.

> *If the doors of perception were cleansed everything would appear to man as it is, Infinite.*
> —William Blake

This first klesha lays the groundwork for suffering by setting up a cascade of false perceptions leading to confusion, misunderstanding, and delusion.

2. **Identification with a false self.** The second klesha is known as *asmita* or "egoism." The ego encompasses our self-image; it's our sense of I, me, my, and mine. Identifying with the positions and possessions of life, the ego is a moment-by-moment artificial construct that creates a rift between that which is me and that which is not.

    This form of suffering isn't possible until we have forgotten the true nature of reality. Once we lose sight of brahman as the unifying principle of oneness and pure consciousness, we create a dualistic split between what we perceive as me "in here" and what is not me "out there." This mistake of the intellect splits the one into many. The split itself isn't the cause of suffering; rather, suffering arises when we confuse our ego for the true self. We believe we're the roles we are playing rather than the one who is portraying a character. It's as if we are wearing a Halloween mask all the time, hiding our true identity from both ourselves and the rest of the world.

By fooling ourselves in this way we create countless opportunities to suffer. We take things personally, we think everything is about us, we believe others are out to take something from us, we generate melodrama and hysteria, we feel superior or inferior to others, we compete rather than cooperate, we're easily offended, we attack others, we judge, criticize, condemn, and complain, we segregate "us" from "them," and find countless ways to separate ourselves from others. As long as we identify with the ego, we are destined to live within a tightly constricted, limited, and isolated center of awareness.

3. **Attachment to objects of desire.** When we forget that we are one with all that is, we begin to believe that the key to happiness lies in getting more *things*. This leads to the pursuit of desire—objects, situations, and relationships that we believe by acquiring will lead to fulfillment or happiness. In the pursuit of these desires however, we often fall into the trap of the third klesha, *raaga*, which means attachment, clinging, or grasping to that which is illusory, impermanent, and unreal.

While the ultimate reality of brahman is eternal, unborn, undying, and infinite, the material level (where we live) is finite, changeable, and *impermanent*. The concept of impermanence is a key principle in the world's great wisdom traditions. It's a sobering truth to recognize that everything on the material level of reality has a beginning, a middle, and an end. Notwithstanding any miraculous medical breakthroughs, within one hundred years, virtually everyone you know will no longer exist on this material level. Buildings, monuments, and mountains will eventually wear away; and on a larger scale, even planets and stars have finite lifetimes.

As much as we might deny the reality of impermanence, at some deep level we all know it to be true. It is this intuitive knowing that compels us to cling, grasp, and become attached to the objects of our desires. Knowing that what we have may be lost creates a deep sense of insecurity, fear, tension, and anxiety. We become inflexible, rigid, and unwilling to change. We attach ourselves to our positions, possessions, our self-image, traditions, cultural influences, ideologies, political beliefs, dogmas, and "the way things have always been" in the hopes of somehow postponing the inevitable change that is a fundamental concept at the heart of our material existence.

Sadly, this clinging and unyielding attachment leads us further down the road of suffering in two key ways. First, it takes an enormous amount of psychological energy to maintain the attachment to your desires. It's as if you are desperately trying to swim upstream against a strong current; you're ultimately fighting the nature of the material universe and doing so will, eventually, leave you exhausted and frustrated. Second, with the understanding that the objects of desire are in the end impermanent, clinging to them essentially becomes an exercise in futility. It's like chasing a shadow. And even if you do catch it, it's only there for a moment before it's gone. So in the end, the harder we cling, the more we suffer.

4. **Aversion or avoiding things we don't want.** At the other end of the attachment spectrum is *dvesha* or "aversion." This is the repulsion or avoidance of those things we don't want in our lives. If you remember the concept of the minefield from Chapter 4, any time something we don't want breaches that ego boundary space, we recoil or try to block the incoming invading influence. If we can't block it, we'll run away—physically, mentally, and/or emotionally.

Aversion is not much different from attachment. It drains our energy and keeps us in a state of worry, anxiety, paranoia, and worst-case scenario thinking. It's essentially a futile exercise though, because no matter how far you retreat from an unwanted influence, you can never get far away enough from what you don't want. Subconsciously, we know this to be true and we're left suffering in fear over what we will do if we can't avoid what we fear most.

5. **The fear of death.** Needing little introduction, the fear of our own personal extinction is without a doubt a foundational cause of suffering for many of us. Know in Sanskrit as *abhinivesha* or "the will to live," this klesha could be considered the ultimate attachment—to that of life itself.

Let's face it, death is the great unknown, and as a rule, human beings aren't so keen on the unknown. Death represents the end of *everything* we know, so it seems only natural to hold on to life and fear its ending. However, the fear of death doesn't apply solely to physical death, but also the death of a situation, a relationship, a rhythm, or a stage of life.

Like attachment, fear of death has its roots sunk deeply into the principle of impermanence. In Sanskrit, the word *anitya* refers to the unstable and inconstant nature of the world. No one intuitively "likes" the idea that the world we live in, all our belongings, our relationships, jobs, and ultimately our most prized and personal possession—our body—will one day no longer exist; however, there is no evidence to the contrary. The specter of death looms a little closer each day and the fear of that eventuality gives birth to all our other fears, anxieties, doubts, and worries.

So now you can see how all of our suffering can be attributed one of the five kleshas. Any time you find yourself caught up in the grip of suffering, pause for a moment and see if you can identify which of the five kleshas is influencing your experience. With a little practice, you'll be able to spot the culprit and perhaps even recognize a pattern. But what then? How can we break this cycle of suffering? Once again, the great sage Patanjali gives us a vital hint in Chapter 2, Sutra 4 of the *Yoga Sutras*: "Ignorance of our real nature is the source of the other four, whether they be dormant, weak, suspended, or fully active."

In other words, the first cause of suffering triggers and enables the remaining four. Without knowing the true nature of reality, we're bumbling around in the dark, destined to be ego driven, attached to and recoiling from things, and petrified of death. However, when we know and understand the true nature of reality as one of oneness, unity, and pure spirt:

1. Our ego no longer runs the show by getting us to buy into its object-referral sense of self-importance, the need to be offended, or desperately seeking the approval of others. We don't destroy or get rid of our ego; instead, we see it for the illusion it is. We can use our ego, but not be controlled by it.
2. We give up the need for attachments to dominate our experience. We recognize impermanence as a foundational part of life. We still have desires, but we don't cling to them. Everything arises, everything fades away, and we're okay with that.
3. We no longer desperately flee or avoid the things we don't want. The comings and goings of life are like a parade of new experiences and in an impermanent universe, we recognize that *this too, shall pass*.
4. We can let go of the fear of death and willingly embrace the unknown. We can recognize death as a transition from one expression of spirit to another. Life becomes liberating and free—a celebration of this short flash of experience between birth and death.

Armed with this understanding, Patanjali continues in Sutras 10-11 of Chapter 2: "The subtle causes of suffering are destroyed when the mind merges back into the unmanifest. The gross effects of suffering are discarded through meditation."

Meditation, therefore, is the key to transcend our suffering. First, meditation creates the witnessing space required to recognize when the kleshas are in play in our lives. Until we identify that the kleshas have us in their grasp, it will be impossible to escape. Being mindful of—and witnessing—your suffering, gives you the space to step back and see through the illusion.

Second, as we've already explored in detail, meditation opens the passageway back to our true selves, helping us remember who we really are. The more frequently we access the ocean of spirit, the more we peel back the layers of "spiritual amnesia" that keep us imprisoned in illusions, egoism, attachment, aversion, and fear. When we wake up to our true nature as infinite beings in an unbounded field of eternal, immortal, invincible, and unlimited consciousness, we can compassionately recognize that we've been doing it to ourselves all along.

Finally, through meditation we can witness and access our *samskaras*, or the subtle mental impressions left by our thoughts, words, and actions. Think of a samskara as a shallow groove cut into a piece of wood. When you pour water over the surface, it naturally flows more easily through the groove than over the rest of the wood. In a similar way, our mental "grooves" are psychological imprints that become the foundation of our habits, patterns of behavior, and life choices. Normally samskaras reside beneath the level of our conscious awareness, but through meditation, we can begin to glimpse their influence over our lives. Once samskaras become conscious, the door is open to conscious choice making. We can course correct and steer away from the patterns, habits of thought, speech, and action that lead to our suffering and navigate back toward the true north of our spirit—the path to liberation, enlightenment, and bliss.

CONCLUSION

We have come to the end of our journey together. We have traveled the Path to Stillness, understood the theory and practice of meditation, explored its countless benefits and rewards, and revealed a map to wellness, self-knowledge, fulfillment, and liberation. But where the map leads is ultimately up to you. I have shown you the territory and given you the keys to the vehicle. Where you go from here is your choice. Will this be the end or just the beginning of an amazing adventure in self-exploration?

As I'm sure you've gathered from these pages, I'm deeply passionate about meditation. And while I freely admit I'm biased, I believe that meditation holds the potential to heal both our individual lives and the world. I'm not saying it's a cure-all, magic bullet. It is, however a tool and practice that can benefit nearly everyone who makes it a regular part of their lives.

And although I've said it before, it bears repeating to remember that all the bountiful benefits of meditation can only be harvested through a regular and consistent practice. Yes, meditating every now and then can bring some stillness and clarity into your life in the short term, but the real magic happens with a committed meditation routine. Make the commitment to a daily practice and you'll find it to be the best gift you've ever given yourself.

Remember, there's no failing in meditation. Every time you sit down to practice, you're giving yourself the deep mind-body rest and reconnection with stillness your soul craves. As we are reminded in the *Bhagavad Gita*, 2:40: "On this path effort never goes to waste, and there is no failure. Even a little effort toward spiritual awareness will protect you from the greatest fear."

For those of you who wish to take the next step in your meditation journey, please see the list of recommended reading and resources in the appendix. Explore the tools and teachings that appeal to you, knowing that your own intuitive guidance will always lead you toward the opportunities and teaching appropriate for your next stage of growth and evolution.

In closing, let me express my deepest gratitude for you not only investing your time and energy in reading this book, but also for investing yourself in the most courageous and noble of all pursuits—the quest to know yourself. Even if you approached meditation for another seemingly less profound reason, meditation is a package deal and through it you have opened the doorway to unlimited possibilities that await your discovery. We are all drawn to meditation when the time is right for us and I am deeply honored to have hopefully provided helpful insight along your journey of awakening. Thank you for allowing me to be your guide and for giving me the opportunity to share my experiences with you. May this knowledge and practice lead you to the fulfillment of all your heart desires.

Peace, harmony, laughter, and love.

APPENDIX

SUGGESTED READING

HIGHLY RECOMMENDED

- *The Seven Spiritual Laws of Success* by Deepak Chopra, MD
- *The Seven Spiritual Laws of Yoga* by Deepak Chopra, MD, and David Simon, MD
- *The Spontaneous Fulfillment of Desire* by Deepak Chopra, MD
- *Secrets of Meditation* by Davidji

CLASSIC VEDANTA AND YOGA PHILOSOPHY

- *The Yoga Sutras of Patanjali* as translated by Alistair Shearer
- *The Crown Jewel of Discrimination* by Adi Shankara
- *The Bhagavad Gita—The Song of God* as translated by Eknath Easwaran

INFORMATION ON THE MAHARISHI EFFECT AND EFFECTS OF GROUP MEDITATION

- *Permanent Peace* by Robert M. Oats
- *Victory Before War* by Robert Keith Wallace and Jay B. Marcus

SCIENTIFIC STUDIES AND RESEARCH ON MEDITATION

- *The Relaxation Response* by Dr. Herbert Benson
- *The Biology of Belief: Unleashing the Power of Consciousness, Matter, & Miracles* by Bruce Lipton
- *The Genie in Your Genes* by Dawson Church PhD
- *Meditation As Medicine: Activate the Power of Your Natural Healing Force* by Dharma Singh Khalsa, MD, and Cameron Stauth
- *Buddha's Brain: The Practical Neuroscience of Happiness, Love, and Wisdom* by Rick Hanson PhD

ADDITIONAL MEDITATION RESOURCES

- *10% Happier* by Dan Harris
- *Mindful Work; How Meditation is Changing Business from the Inside Out* by David Gelles
- *How to Meditate* by Lawrence LeShan
- *Meditation* by Eknath Easwaran
- *Strength In the Storm* by Eknath Easwaran
- *Wherever You Go, There You Are* by John Kabat-Zinn
- *Healing Mantras* by Thomas Ashley-Farrand

GUIDED MEDITATION CDS

- *Chakra Balancing; Body, Mind and Soul* by Deepak Chopra
- *davidji—Guided Meditations* by davidji
- *Sacred Chants CD* featuring Beth Nielsen Chapman
- *Mantras and Music* - Music from the Chopra Center's 21-Day Meditation Challenge

NOTES

CHAPTER 5

1 Jeremy Smith, "The Perils of Multitasking," *ChurchMag*, August 31, 2012, https://churchm.ag/the-perils-of-multitasking/.

CHAPTER 6

1 Robert M. Oates, *Permanent Peace: How to Stop Terrorism and War—Now and Forever* (Fairfield, IA: Institute of Science, Technology & Public Policy, 2002).

2 Robert Keith Wallace and Jay B. Marcus, *Victory Before War: Preventing Terrorism through the Vedic Peace Technologies of His Holiness Maharishi Mahesh Yogi* (Fairfield, IA: Maharishi University of Management Press, 2005).

3 Deepak Chopra and David Simon, *The Seven Spiritual Laws of Yoga: A Practical Guide to Healing Body, Mind, and Spirit* (Hoboken, NJ: John Wiley & Sons, 2004).

CHAPTER 7

1 Deepak Chopra, "Awaken Your Creative Response," *The Chopra Center*, November 20, 2012, https://chopra.com/articles/awaken-your-creative-response.

CHAPTER 9

1 Deepak Chopra, *The Seven Spiritual Laws of Success: A Practical Guide to the Fulfillment of Your Dreams* (San Rafael, CA: Amber-Allen Publishing; Novato, CA: New World Library, 1993).

CHAPTER 10

1 Bruce H. Lipton, *The Biology of Belief: Unleashing the Power of Consciousness, Matter & Miracles* (Santa Rosa, CA: Mountain of Love/Elite Books, 2005), https://www.brucelipton.com/.

MEDITATION LOG

Date	Time	Location	Experience

Date	Time	Location	Experience

ACKNOWLEDGEMENTS

No book is written in a void, and what on the surface appears to be the work of one person is always a collaboration of support, inspiration, or influence from countless individuals. Without the direct or indirect assistance of the following people, this book would never have come to be. First and foremost, to Dana Brady, who not only supports me in my crazy ideas, but somehow resonates with me on so many levels. To the work and teachings of the co-founders of the Chopra Center for Wellbeing, Deepak Chopra and David Simon – your inspiration continues to light the way for so many seeking deeper expressions of health, happiness, and fulfillment. To my extended Chopra Center Family of fellow instructors – you have worked diligently to help these teachings thrive in your own unique way as well as inspired me to continue to learn, grow, and reach for my highest potential – Roger Gabriel, Teresa Long, Erica Lopez, Claire Diab, Amanda Ree, Rene Ringnalda, Libby Carstensen, Tris Thorp, and Melissa Eisler. To the meditation force of nature, Davidji for trailblazing a path of higher awareness throughout the world and taking the time to write the amazing forward of this book. To the teachers who inspired me as a college student to study and explore the world's great wisdom traditions – Alan Watts, Ram Dass, Jiddu Krishnamurti, Joseph Campbell, Paramahansa Yogananda, and Bruce Lee. A deep bow to fellow martial artists, instructors, and friends who took the time to read and review the manuscript: JB Jaeger, Jonathan Burke, Laura Giancarlo, John Giancarlo, Dr. Rodney

Dunetz, Kate Miller, Harinder Singh Sabharwal, and Melissa Feldman – your keen eyes and helpful feedback mean more than you know. To my incredible Wellness Family – your leadership and friendship has been and continues to be a source of great joy in my life – Sarah Popiel, Cheryl Owens, Susan Mickelson, Kimberly Sheerin, Lauren Klyczek, Alex Eischen and Lisa Phillips. To Steve Miles – your support and flexibility has allowed me to take these teachings to the people who need them the most. To Rac Po – for being a great office partner, friend, and sounding board. To my editorial and publishing team at *Author Imprints* – Katie Barry and David Wogahn – your knowledge and expertise has been indispensable to this publishing noob. To all my students, new, returning, and the DRC Back Row – your dedication to these teachings keeps me coming back year after year. And lastly, but certainly not least, to the Source of all that is, was, and will be – thanks for downloading this stuff through me and letting me be an instrument of peace to the best of my ability.

>Tat Tvam Asi; *through the mirror of relationship, I discover my true self.*

Thank you all!

ABOUT THE AUTHOR

Chopra Center Vedic Educator, Certified Meditation, Yoga, Mind-Body Wellness Instructor, and Martial Artist, Adam Brady has been a lifetime seeker of spiritual and transcendent wisdom. A practicing meditator for over two decades, he is the author of *Warrior of Light, A Martial Art Fable* and over 50 published articles on meditation, yoga, and mind-body health. Adam is dedicated to helping people transform their lives through a consciousness-based approach to living and for over a decade he has been sharing his passion for meditation with hundreds of private and corporate clients, helping them tap into their own potential for stillness, peace, transformation, and healing.

For additional information, visit **www.revisedreality.com**

ALSO BY ADAM BRADY

Emulating the ideal that true understanding and awareness in a spiritually evolved martial artist has the ability to transform the world, this story shares a unique and profound message of epic proportions. Deeply moving, *Warrior of Light* is a martial arts fantasy fiction with a powerful and universal message of strength, spirituality, and resilience.

www.ingramcontent.com/pod-product-compliance
Lightning Source LLC
Chambersburg PA
CBHW020441110526
44587CB00038B/773